Dad Notes

Some Stuff You Oughta Know

Lon K. Riley

COPYRIGHT

Photography and Cover Art by Ashley Riley.

First Paperback Printing, November 2020.
ISBN: 979-85-56644-94-6

For a Son

TABLE OF CONTENTS

PREFACE

It's been almost twenty years, but I remember with vivid clarity, sitting in a dark corner rocking a baby to sleep in his room. Every night, I would feed him a bottle and then put him on my shoulder and sit in that corner by the window, rocking him to sleep. I would wonder where this little guy would go and what he would do. I would consider how I would handle the challenge of raising him the right way and setting him up for success. Then, I would generally worry about all of it.

One of the things I worried about most was something happening that would prevent me from being there for him and teaching him all of the things he would need to know. An event that would prevent me from providing him with the tools to become a successful and productive adult. I feel like I can't possibly be alone. Leaving a child with no guidance must be a chief worry amongst parents who care about their children's success. So, what could I do about it?

I was fortunate to have a pretty good upbringing in a stable home with great parents. We were not well off by any means, but I had it good. I had it way better than many and understand now how this structure alone can set you up for future success. One of the most pivotal moments of my life was my mother's loss when

I was 18 and just getting started in college. About a month into my freshman year in college, she had a massive stroke, which we found out soon after was related to a brain tumor. After being bed-ridden with almost no ability to communicate or function on her own for nearly a year, she passed. This series of events had a tremendous impact on me, which probably goes without saying, but it affected me in ways I did not understand until much later.

I primarily came to understand the deep-rooted fear of sudden loss and a little bit of a fear of success. My parents went through a lot in the years before my mom's stroke. They had managed to navigate the kids through school while taking on new careers and higher education of their own. I always felt like things were just on the brink of getting good for them when the hammer fell. It took a while to realize, but these feelings manifested themselves in me as a kind of fear of success. I lived in fear of things getting too good, for fear of the bad that ultimately comes next. This example certainly illustrates how early influence can alter a kid's perception of future events. The reality is that the good and bad come and go as time passes, so dwelling on the mere possibilities of the bad doesn't make a whole lot of sense and can bring you down. Nonetheless, I still dwell on the negative sometimes, and one of those deep-rooted fears is something happening to me and leaving the kid behind unprepared and vulnerable.

From experience, I understand that everything can change most drastically, out of the blue, on a Tuesday in September. It has been many years since I lost my mother, and I recall the feeling of helplessness when having a question for her and, wow, there are no answers.

So, we have the premise for this book. I know a little bit about a lot of stuff. I have also done some stuff. I have done some smart stuff, but more exceptionally dumb stuff and just about everything in between. I have probably made every mistake in the proverbial book. We call them "life lessons" in our household and, to be honest, I am tired of life lessons. I wish I just had all of the answers, and finally, things would be so much easier and less frustrating. Unfortunately, that's not the way this life thing works, and I have learned, in no small degree, to embrace the value of the mistakes I have made.

My son is an adult now, and my wife and I have done what we can to set him up for success. We feel like we have raised a reasonably confident and intelligent person who is socially conscious and self-aware. I may be wrong, but let's go with it until proven differently. Still, we have gaps. He said to me a while back, "man, I'm getting ready to move out to a different state, and there are so many things I don't know." This kind of hit home because it means, despite my best efforts over time, there is still so much information that I have yet to pass down. I was kicking the ideas for this book around for years and had written many notes, mostly coherent (again, let's go with that) but still largely fragmented. So, I finally decided to put pen to paper, so to speak, to pull this information together and perhaps answer many of the questions he will have in the pages of this book. If the information and advice can work for him, it may work for others.

There are tons of kids who did not have nearly the head start my son or I had. I was listening to a podcast the other day discussing the "negativity effect," and it was relevant to this topic for a couple of reasons. First, there is the premise that people have a tendency to dwell on the negative and that those types of events in life have significantly more impact on future perspectives than the positive. Of course, that has been part of my challenge, and when you think about that, it sounds obvious. When you consider this dynamic, it can help you understand and reshape your thinking. In the context of this particular podcast discussion, the author made the point that in the process of raising a child, the upside of being a great parent is not nearly as impactful as the downside of being a bad parent or an absentee parent. That is, to succeed at being a parent or guardian, you don't have to be great; you just have to be there and be "not bad." I am still not sure I am in 100% agreement with that premise, but I found it interesting and relevant to what I am trying to accomplish here.

So, enter the Dad Notes concept. I suppose this could be called Parent or Guardian Notes, and of course, no disrespect to the Moms out there. But I am a Dad, and these are my notes. The goal here is to provide a subset of useful information to young adults in a context that delivers thoughtful direction but still inspires them to think for themselves. I hope that much of the information will reconcile with the adults who then pass this book onto those who may benefit from it.

Many of the topics and tenets discussed here are indisputable, like "start saving early". Anyone who opposes that opinion should probably choose a different book because you are unlikely to appreciate the rest of the very pragmatic stuff. I also sprinkle in a whole lot of advice based on my opinion and life experience. I designed and wrote this book with junior high, high school, early college-age folks in mind. This age presents a time in life in which information can be lacking, and it is hard to ask for help but easy to get into trouble. It is also easy to slip into the wrong habits or in the wrong direction. Just having a head start with some things to think about and watch out for can help those in this age group avoid the pitfalls that could damage them severely and hurt their chances of success later in life.

The guidance provided here is straightforward and delivered intentionally, without any social, economic, political, religious, or ethnic slant. It is merely sensible, rational information, written from my perspective, to help those who may benefit from it. However, I understand fully that all of the content here will not reconcile with everyone, so I have left room for notes at the end of each chapter. The printed edition is easy enough to write in, and most electronic versions will allow you to enter notes and highlight sections, as well.

I hope that folks can use this work "as-is", for anyone from teen to young adult who could use some fatherly advice on key topics that could significantly impact their immediate and future success and well-being. For those parents, guardians, or mentors who want to review this first and put their spin on it, please do; that is the design. It took me years to finally sit down and make this happen, and it was hard. So, rather than writing your own book, start with this one and use it as the basis for your teaching. If you disagree with something, write it down and explain why. If you feel a section or thought is pure genius or even just "not bad," take a moment and reinforce any ideas with your thoughts or notes. If you don't feel like writing, talk about it. Any way you decide to approach it, your kids will appreciate it.

ACKNOWLEDGEMENTS

I would like to thank Ashley and Keegan for their support and encouragement during this project, as well as all of the great family, friends, bosses, co-workers, and even a few strangers who have pulled me off of the edge over and over again. You know who you are. Maybe this returns the favor in some way.

I also have to thank all of the people who put me down, wasted my time, scammed me, yelled at me, threatened me, sued me, pushed me around, lied to me, and almost killed me. I could not have done this without you.

INTRODUCTION

"Before every expedition, my Dad tells me to "Be bold, be safe, be smart." This has turned into a mantra that I repeat while exhausted on big climbs."

~ Graham Zimmerman

Before we get to the sage wisdom that I will shortly bestow upon you, I would like to cover a few elements related to the concept and construct of this book. I use "sage wisdom" tongue-in-cheek here, of course. If you read the preface, you understand that the primary motivation is to give some guidelines and general advice based on my experience, which will benefit you and keep you safe and healthy. Some advice that can help you build a great starting point for handling what the world throws at you. You may even make a few bucks or save a few bucks and avoid some aggravation.

That said, the big theme I want you to take away from this book and into life is that you are solely responsible for yourself. Take all advice and information (including this) for what it is - data points based upon someone else's opinion and life experience. People love to talk about themselves and, as a result, you will find throughout your life that you will be taking in information from many people and sources. Some information will be invaluable, some total rubbish, and most of it somewhere in between. Everyone has an experience and an opinion. Being smack in the middle of the information age here, you have data and opinions coming at you from all sides. If someone has an idea or an opinion they want to put out there, it is as easy as recording a 30-second video and uploading it to social media, and it is out there for the world. Valid or invalid, sound or ridiculous, it is there for you to process.

There is information that is disseminated, right or wrong, with the best intentions. There is also the information out there designed specifically to exploit you, control you, confuse you, separate you from your money, or for any number of other nefarious reasons.

Consider your sources. Should you be taking medical advice from a blogger? Financial, investment, or legal advice from a social media acquaintance? No matter how much you trust them, are they qualified to dole out this information? Is the person giving you the advice financially or otherwise personally motivated by the decision you make? If so, you need to be even more careful in evaluating the data and information.

So why would you take any advice from me? I'm glad you asked. In short, because I've been around for a while, and I've screwed some stuff up. I mean really screwed some stuff up. I am finalizing this intro piece as the last step in writing this book, and, as I browse the table of contents, I realize that maybe four chapters are written from the perspective of when I actually got it right the first time. For the rest of the chapters, the experience is based upon the screw-ups. Whether getting it right or getting it wrong, the important thing is that you learn from it. I have learned a few things along the way, and I hope you can benefit from my painful learning curve.

I have always felt that if someone is kind enough to stop and take the time to provide me with some insights, I should probably at least spend a moment evaluating the information. I would recommend you do the same. But never be afraid to take a step back and slow the process. There are very few split-second decisions you will ever have to make in life, and absolutely none of those involve buying something, signing a contract, or otherwise making a commitment. If you are making a decision in haste and based upon limited information, you will probably end up making a costly mistake. Think about that hot stock that will never be available at this low price again. That person who demands you do something you are uncomfortable with, or they will not be your friend. That "once in a lifetime" deal on something you want to buy that makes you sure you have to act *right now.*

Here is a secret, the next deal is right around the corner, always. So is the next great stock pick or the next great friend. You're not missing out on anything by taking a little time and objectively evaluating the information you receive before making decisions. You will save yourself a lot of aggravation and headache by assessing your options and making controlled, sound decisions based upon facts and not strictly upon pure emotion.

I have tried to keep the information written here to just the facts as I see them - information for you to take in and evaluate, analyze, and consider.

Ultimately, with everything in life, you have to think and act for yourself — question everything. Seek out the data points and aggregate them. Process them to develop a deep understanding. That goes for the content of this book as well. I have accumulated some opinions based upon my experience that I am choosing to share with you, hoping that it will help you somehow. I encourage you to consider this information, but as with any information you encounter...take the time to think about it, evaluate it, research it before making potentially life-changing decisions based upon it.

All that said, I have designed the information provided here to make you think and consider some concepts. I have included a list of resources throughout, where appropriate, and additional recommendations in the final chapter. These are reference points I have come across over the years that I have used to shape my world view, gain experience in certain areas, or help me get out of a bind. The information given here will not make you an expert on any one topic. It will merely provide you the direction to explore, gain additional knowledge and expertise, and form your opinions for yourself.

There is some mildly uncomfortable subject matter discussed here but hang with it because it is invaluable to help you avoid the bad stuff and keep you alive, out of trouble, and thinking for yourself. We will also spend a lot of time on the good stuff. Some things that will help make you healthier, happier, more productive, and ultimately set you up for success.

An ounce of prevention is better than a pound of cure. In other words, you're better off avoiding the pitfalls than having to fix the problems later.

Many of you will read these chapters and think, "I wish someone had told me this sooner," because you've been through some of these things already or feel trapped in situations as a result of similar circumstances. For this reason, I have also sprinkled in some advice in these particular sections that could help. Don't be discouraged, even if you are currently in a rough situation — quite the opposite.

Everyone starts from a different place. Everyone makes mistakes, some more difficult to overcome than others, but anyone can overcome them. The sin is not in making mistakes. The sin is failing to own your mistakes and learn from them, then possibly even repeating them as a result. And always remember, you can overcome anything with the right mentality and support system. Whatever you do, don't give up. Ever.

IMPRESSIONS

"I am trying to impress myself. I have yet to do it."

~ Shia LeBoeuf

Many of the actions we take every day are driven by attempts to impress others, consciously, or unconsciously. It is easy for me to say never try to impress others, only seek to impress yourself. I suppose this is good advice and something to aspire to, but that is more like a lifelong journey than a simple decision you can make one day and consistently carry out.

When you seek to impress someone else, your motive is acceptance, a deep-rooted psychological facet of the human species. We all want to be accepted. We all want to be part of a group, part of something bigger than ourselves.

This type of acceptance goes for family life, work-life, friend life, and it is essential to understand there is nothing wrong with this. We are continually seeking that group of like-minded individuals who help support us and round out our lives. Seeking acceptance by making the right impression is a simple fact of life, but you need to carefully consider a few things.

In an attempt to impress, try to evaluate who exactly you are trying to impress and why. Think about the people from whom you are seeking acceptance and evaluate - is this the type of person you want to be?

Seeking acceptance is a theme you will repeatedly see from grade school through your professional working life. The group of guys who hang around and smoke weed all day think you're pretty cool and want you to join them. Will you join them, so they think you're cool too? Think about why and what comes next. The more this group accepts you, the deeper you are drawn in, and you may eventually become just like them. Is this really what you want, or does it compromise your integrity, values, and goals?

In the professional world, it works the same way. I worked with law firms for several years. Many of the very highly paid managing partners were the types that would yell and degrade employees and even peers. Their mentors had taught them that this is the way to act if they wanted to get ahead and be successful. I would see some of the junior partners start to take on these character traits.

In many cases, I could tell this is not who these people truly are at their core. But they would raise their voices and degrade quickly when in the managing partners' presence, to curry favor and get ahead. It was pretty sad to see them compromise their core values to impress someone they thought could advance their careers. They did the "right" things to impress the "right" people and, in doing so, lost a lot of themselves. I am sure they made a lot of money in the process, but the cost of this type of advancement is always high, too. I also know a lot of attorneys who made just as much money, or even more, and treated their staff members with respect. They also had some fun along the way.

I am not in any way saying to avoid making a good impression on the right people by putting your best foot forward. Just because you prefer sandals to shoes, and you feel this represents you as a person, it does not mean you should wear beach sandals to your job interview at the bank. You can seek measured acceptance and still conform to societal norms where appropriate, without losing sight of yourself. Seek always acceptance with autonomy. Wear your shoes to work and switch right back to sandals when you get home. You can always choose to impress through impressive actions, not those that compromise who you are and who you want to be.

If you set your standards high and seek to impress yourself daily, through your actions and thoughts, you will end up in the right place.

<u>Notes:</u>

SCHOOL

*"If a man empties his purse into his head,
no man can take it away from him. An
investment in knowledge always pays the
best interest."*

~ Benjamin Franklin

Education is a gift, and you should choose to treat it that way, pursuing life-long learning in whatever you decide to do. In many developed world countries, primary education is free and available to almost everyone, which is remarkable. Some schools are much better than others, to be sure, but the infrastructure is there for learning if you choose to pursue it.

It seems so simple, do your Kindergarten through Grade 12, because you kind of have to - then make some sort of decisions. You can follow a college path and then maybe graduate school.

Perhaps go straight into the "real world" and get a job, start a business, go to trade school, any number of things.

So many young people stress hard about "what am I going to do with my life." The awesome reality is that you don't have to know. You will not have all of the answers, or maybe any of the answers, at 18 years old. I am almost 50 years old and not entirely sure what I will be doing in two years, but I know that I will continue to grow and learn and that education will light the way. Following a path of lifelong education will lead you in the right direction. Taking school seriously and following a few simple guidelines will set you up for success in whatever you end up doing.

Initially, I began writing this chapter specifically about college. But so many people take so many different paths. College is not right for many people, for any number of reasons, but everyone will deal with at least junior high and high school. Beyond that, many careers require certifications, trade schools, licensing, or other ongoing education. The principles are all the same, and if you choose a path of lifelong learning, participating in education will continue to come back around in some form or fashion. These guidelines will help you to frame up success in whichever educational path you take.

I went to college at Tulane University in New Orleans, and, admittedly, I was a pretty terrible student in the first few years. I did not know a lot of this stuff and tried to take the easy way out, opting out of optional assignments and homework, not showing up for class, cramming at the last minute for exams, and making basically all of the mistakes listed here. As a result, my grade point average (GPA) early on was horrendous. I pulled it up eventually, but never to the level I would have liked. I set myself up early on for later struggles and could never achieve the level of success I would have if I had gone in and done it the right way. I will recount some stories here that show what a desperately underprepared sap I was entering college. Hopefully, you will avoid the same traps in junior high or high school, and beyond in whatever educational path you choose to pursue.

I recently met with a college professor, and we were discussing this very same topic. He told me that in his experience, a 2.5 GPA college graduate would take around *ten years* to get to the same salary a 3.5+ GPA student will earn directly out of college. Think about that. And he's right - I had a remarkable senior year at Tulane, but only after many years of tough times and abysmal grades. I was able to pull up my GPA, but not to a level that would afford me many options. I guarantee it took ten years to start earning what many of my compatriots began with right out of college.

That's the thing with grades, which is so important. When you have good grades, you have options. When you have poor grades, those options shrink up dramatically. In high school, the difference between a 2.5 GPA and a 3.5 GPA means a very different set of choices. At 3.5 +, you can gain acceptance to many different colleges and maybe even get scholarship money, which will significantly expand your options. At 2.5, you may or may not even get into the colleges you like, let alone gain any money toward education. Unless you are wealthy, if you want to go to college, this can be the difference between going right into college and working for many years first. The principle is the same for certificates, trade schools, on-the-job training, or other continuing education. You put in the work and get the marks, and your options open up. Here's how to do it.

Show Up

It sounds so simple, but just showing up to class is perhaps the most significant measure of future success and many people don't do it. The reasons vary as widely as any other excuse for not doing what you're supposed to do. I don't like the instructor; it's boring, I already know the material, I want to have fun doing something else, the class is early, and I oversleep. Go ahead, pick your lame excuse - but I will give you a bunch of reasons you need to show up, regardless of what story you have manufactured to the contrary. Oh, and please show up on time, every time. Being on time is essential for classes and everything else.

First, being present in class every time builds your habit. You have to get into the rhythm and get into the subject matter. Without rhythm, you have a constant set of stops and restarts. The materials you already learned will evaporate, and you continuously have to start over again, refreshing things you have already reviewed. It wastes a lot more time than if you show up and get those pieces consistently ingrained in your mind.

Next, showing up demonstrates to the instructor that you care about the subject matter and the value of their time teaching it, *whether you care or not.* Your instructor is the person who will hand you the grade at the end of the course, semester or year, and it would be wise not to alienate them or degrade their profession. You may be a math person and find English class boring and useless. I assure you the instructor who has chosen English as the path for their career does not feel the same way. If you view education as a gift, as I started the chapter with, you can reframe that mentality and spend your time learning something that will serve you well in the future. Even mathematicians need to read and write effectively.

Finally, and this should come as no surprise, you're going to learn something when you show up. I used to go fishing with this guy "down the bayou" in Southern Louisiana, and he would always say, "You got to go, to know." What he meant was, we would sit around and speculate on whether or not the fish would be there due to weather, tides, bait, whatever. The reality is you have to go to find out. Same with class. Even if it is boring and slow, or you know the subject matter - you are going to pick up something. There are so many aspects to the class setting and "You got to go, to know" - new assignments, changes to materials, quiz and test dates, updates on projects, or information that frames subject context that you cannot get from notes. You could rely on friends or classmates to tell you, but what have we already learned about that? You are solely responsible for yourself, and when you start relying on other people's notes and recollections, you can only hope that they were paying attention and that they understood.

Do the Work

All of the work. Again, this sounds too simple, but the biggest mistakes people make are not completing *optional* assignments and waiting until the last minute to "cram." Optional assignments often contain specific information that instructors use to reinforce for quizzes or exams. And cramming is a colossal mistake, never works, and will not net you the success you will find by just doing the work regularly and making steady progress. I had two very different next-door neighbors in the dorms at Tulane during my freshman year, one on each side of me. The first, a guy who I have not seen since we moved out of the dorms, went to every class, did every assignment. He studied for a little while every evening, while many of us were off fooling around. The night before an exam, he would stop studying (usually before the rest of us would even start) and relax. He was never stressed and always carried As. I can only assume he was extremely successful in anything he did professionally.

Now, on the other side of me was a whole different story. This guy is a dude who was also never stressed, but that was just his personality type. He was also admittedly lazy, although extremely intelligent. I recall him coming back from his first Organic Chemistry class and telling us the "good news" - you could not do any assignments the whole semester, or even take the mid-term exam, and just take the final exam for your entire semester grade. I vividly remember the conversation when he said he would not go to the class anymore, but I legitimately thought he was joking. He was not joking. The night before the final exam, we were there when he unwrapped the textbook from its packaging. He had not opened the book yet. He then sat there for 3-4 hours, flipping through pages, while watching TV. He got a C on the exam, which is actually quite remarkable.

The point of this story is not to show that you can be lazy and still not fail. He clearly had some prior knowledge of the subject matter and is quite a brilliant guy. Very, very few people could pull this off with a grade other than a low F. In this scenario, he was fine with achieving the minimum needed to get by, and that is also a big mistake. He could have done just a little bit of work, shown up to class and done basic exercises, and blown it away with an A. We're still good friends today, and, as much as this has become an amusing anecdote 30 years later, he would agree that it would have been wise to start that freshman year with a bunch of easy As rather than only slightly easier Cs. He had the same struggles later that I had, having to work twice as hard to pull up his GPA to get the job he wanted. You can save some effort on the front end, but it will cost you dearly on the back end.

Understand the Work

Doing the work is one thing, and understanding it is another. And I don't mean surface-level understanding, but a deep understanding of the principles, not just the facts.

One of the other mistakes we would make as college newcomers were with the open note test. This example is comical how stupid we were. Some of the instructors would let us bring in one page of notes to exams. We would spend hours upon hours making one-page cheat sheets with tiny writing so that we could cram as much information on the page as possible.

I remember being in the exams and not even finding the information I was looking for on the cheat sheet because the writing was so tiny, and I could not remember where I put it. It would have made a lot more sense for us to spend the same amount of time developing an understanding of the material than writing ridiculous notes to cheat the system. Remember my next-door neighbor who did the work every day? His sheet would have 8-10 equations on it, and I am not sure he even used it. He had As every time versus my Cs and Ds.

Build Instructor Relationships

I learned far too late the value of relationships, especially relationships with those driving the subject matter and generating the grades. As a senior at Tulane, I had sorted out the three subjects above (finally) and was doing exceptionally well. I was in class and engaged, doing the work, getting excellent grades, and finding this was way better than cramming and being stressed all the time. I took a graduate-level class based primarily on the C computer programming language. I had minimal prior experience with C, and this was not a required class. I went to the instructor before the semester began to express my concerns. Even though

I liked the subject matter, I was concerned I would not keep up, as the other students had extensive prior knowledge that I lacked. He assured me we would learn the language and programming throughout the class. I recall the sinking feeling as, at the end of session number 3, a class session in which I understood next to nothing, and he said, "well, that's the end of our primer of C, let's get started on the projects." I was screwed.

Rather than quitting, though, which I could have done, I decided that I had something to prove here and would make it happen. I was attached to two graduate students who were extremely well versed in the programming piece, and our group of three set out to do this large data processing project. I worked harder than you can imagine to keep-up and contribute. Although I am sure they went back and rewrote many of my contributions, they knew I was giving it my best effort. I went to the instructor's office during office hours every week with questions that needed clarification. Through this process, I realized the value of these interactions. Not only was I mining valuable data from an expert in this subject matter, but it showed him how hard I was working and that I was asking the right questions. These meetings led to at least a half-point bump in my grade at the end of the semester. As a result, I adopted this across all classes, asking pointed, clarifying questions directly of the instructor, and developing meaningful relationships through discussion. Take full advantage of instructor office hours. Ask great questions, and make sure they know who you are and that you are working hard to master their subject matter.

Stay Ahead

Do not wait until the last minute. I feel like I preface every bullet point in this chapter with, "this is obvious" or "it sounds so simple," but bad habits are so easy to slip into, and procrastination is a silent killer. It is so easy to let things slide and slide until you are stuck racing at the last minute or pulling an all-nighter. Not only does this create undue stress, but your work product also will not be anywhere near what it could be if completed thoughtfully, in an appropriate amount of time. My advice here is to make steady progress, a little bit of effort across all subjects or projects, every day. If you put in even minimal effort on days that you really don't feel like it and then work a little harder when you have the energy and focus, things will come together. This technique works with studying and projects, both of which you will encounter in any educational path you pursue and in the professional world.

<u>Notes:</u>

TIME AND FOCUS

*"Concentrate all your thoughts upon the
work at hand. The sun's rays do not burn
until brought to a focus."*

~ Alexander Graham Bell

It is essential to designate time to focus on specific projects and things you need to accomplish. Committing to focus time is especially important given the world we live in right now, where information is flying at you from all angles, all the time. You already deal with constant stimulation and distraction, primarily now in the form of mobile phones and the internet.

To direct your focus and absorb and process information effectively, you must carve out time in which you limit or even eliminate distractions and focus on one key thing at a time.

For many years, professionals viewed multitasking as the ultimate in productivity. People capable of multitasking were the real "go-getters" who could get things done. Anything you throw at them, they tick a box and throw it right back.

What we have learned over the years is that multitasking is mostly ineffective. Continually shifting gears between projects, tasks, subjects, or priorities takes away from the deeper focus required to do effective and meaningful work in a reasonable amount of time. It also hurts your ability to retain critical information in a study setting. The solution is to block off dedicated focus time to complete the most vital and complicated work.

On the subject of time, there is a phrase that you should be familiar with that was coined by the 20th-century British scholar named C. Northcote Parkinson. It is referred to as Parkinson's law and states that "work expands so as to fill the time available for its completion." The premise is that if you designate, for example, one hour to complete a project that should take 15 minutes, that project will likely drag out to fill the full hour. You may not be of the age yet where you have attended many work meetings, but in the professional world, scheduled meetings can be a real productivity killer. You schedule a meeting for an hour to review a new policy, for example. Everyone drags into a conference room, fixes coffee, chats about their weekend or their kids. 15 minutes in, and the meeting starts. People come in late, and people drift off to take calls. Everyone feels compelled to be in the room for the full hour, even though the actual policy review took just a few minutes, and everyone agreed — total waste of time.

This type of dynamic can occur with individual focus, too. You carve out an hour to do your math homework. Fifteen minutes in, and you are half-way done. You are now way ahead of schedule. Maybe pop over and check email, see if anyone has hit you up on Snapchat. Respond to a few messages, send some selfies of you "studying." Open a web browser, see a popup, read an article. Send a few texts. Oops - the hour is up, and you only finished half of what you set out to do. Or, maybe you finished it all but could have knocked out science and English, too, in the same amount of time.

In developing my focus time routine, I have considered both the "focus" and the "time," coming up with a simple system that helps drive focus without letting the work expand to fill the time. I have found this simple routine works well for work environments, school studying, or even home projects. I have come up with a few fundamental rules to follow. If you can manage to carve out focus time blocks in your day, you will see your overall productivity increase and have more free time.

Establish Your Focus Time Schedule

This may be the most challenging part of the process, and I get it. If you are in school and juggling classes, homework, sports, band, or other practice, and still want to get together with friends when things come up, this is hard. In the working world, you may have to deal with a demanding boss and shifting priorities, so carving out dedicated time on the calendar and sticking to it can be very difficult. I handle it at work by putting two 1-hour focus time blocks on my calendar every day and marking them as "busy" to keep people from scheduling meetings with me during these times.

If you are a student or younger member of the workforce, you may have to get more creative or even do some focused time after hours, mornings, or evenings. Irrespective of how you choose to block out your time, the most important thing is to commit to the block. Even if it changes day to day, when the opportunity arises to block some time, take advantage of it, and follow the steps below. The other thing to remember is that if you have a dynamic schedule, it is ok if things change if blocks get missed. This process should help you dial in and focus, not become another goal that creates stress.

Eliminate All Distractions

And I mean all distractions. There are a few you probably don't even consider. First, you need to carve out a productive place to sit and work. Establish a work area with a clean desk or table, a door that closes, or other quiet space like a study or work cubicle. If you have to use a public place like a library or coffee shop, try to find a quiet corner where you will not be distracted by people you know or others in conversation. The most significant potential for distraction is the mobile phone. I would recommend just setting your device to silent and placing it in a drawer or work bag where you will not look at it until your focus time is complete.

Turn off the TV or any other visual distraction, and if you are working on your computer, close all internet browser screens to prevent any popups. Many of us also use other chat functions on computers, and these should all be closed, so they don't pop up and indicate new messages to which you may review or even respond.

Email is a massive distraction for most people, especially in a work environment. I have eliminated all popup email notifications, not just during focus time, but all the time. The temptation to read and respond to every email that pops up is a constant distraction and productivity killer. At a minimum, turn off all notifications during focus time, and turn them back on if you prefer when the time block is complete.

Prepare Your To-Do List in Advance

This is a big one to prevent the task expansion we discussed earlier and make the best use of your time, based on how you prefer to work. I have two different styles of focus time blocks; creative time and task-based time. I am more creative in the morning hours and will typically use the morning to advance creative work like writing. I also have lots of task-based work that can be a little more mindless but needs to be done - paying the bills, contacting vendors, reading contracts, signing checks, that kind of stuff. I keep a master list of task priorities that are in the queue. I may dedicate a focus time block to a significant creative project or direct my time toward the task-based work. Typically, I block creative in the morning and task-based in the afternoons, when my creativity wanes and energy is a little lower. You have to carve out what is right for you and not be afraid to shift gears based on the situation. There are mornings I head into a writer's block (pun intended), and I'm just not feeling it, or the ideas are not coming. I may pull out the to-do list and continue to work the focus time with task-based items. Or, I may scrap the block entirely if the timing and the feeling are not right. Remember, this is about focusing on productivity, so I will not sit and stare at a computer screen only to accomplish nothing for an hour.

When it comes to the task-based time blocks, it is essential to have more than one thing lined up and not to tie a particular task to an amount of time. Instead, work the list one item at a time to completion, based on your priorities, then move on to the next. Accomplish as many things as you can in the allotted time and when it is time to stop, just stop and reset your list for the next focus block.

In whichever manner you decide to structure your focus system, the point is to maximize your time by focusing effort and limiting distractions.

<u>Notes:</u>

DRINKING, DRUGS, AND PARTYING

*"Selling my soul would be a lot easier if I
could just find it."*

*~ Nikki Six, The Heroin Diaries: A
Year in the Life of a Shattered Rock Star*

We're going to dive right in now to some difficult subject matter. I placed this chapter relatively early in the book here because it is critically important that you are conscious of these pitfalls if you want to have any chance of being a successful and productive person.

This chapter was easy to write because I have plenty of years of experience (directly and indirectly) with all of the above, and I have seen some tragic stuff go down as a result. Thinking about it now, I have come very close to going lights-out myself due to drugs or alcohol at least seven times that I can recollect. Some were the pure result of other people's stupidity and my just being in the wrong place at the wrong time. However, a few were related directly to my own poor decisions and putting myself into bad situations through one or more of the ways described herein. These are the real cringe-worthy ones - those that I could have avoided by just thinking and following the basic guidelines I will give you here.

None of this is meant simply to scare you. Well, some of it is - and it should scare you because it's all true. I want you to think about the choices you may face and start to process these scenarios now, hopefully before you are in the middle of them. If you are already in the middle of a situation with drugs or alcohol, keep reading. This section is for you, too, and you can get out.

Drugs and alcohol will alter your state of consciousness, the way you think that drives your actions. The long and short of taking any substance that alters your state of consciousness is that your ability to make sound decisions will become impaired. Not only will you think and act slower, but you will also do so without the critical decision-making capability that your brain uses to keep you safe, healthy, and, most importantly, alive. Think about this stuff now, play out the scenarios, and arm yourself with the knowledge to act accordingly when confronted.

This might seem like really uncomfortable stuff to read, and I am pretty direct about it, but give it a go and hang with it. The chapter is short, but perhaps the most crucial chapter in the book. The reason is, every single thing here is avoidable if you can understand the scenarios and abide by a few guidelines. There are also a few things you have probably never heard before.

Let's start with the easy one, Drugs. When it comes to this subject, the statement that "everything is ok in moderation" is a total fallacy.

Never, For Any Reason, Should You Ingest;

- Illegal Drugs, in any form.
- Someone else's prescription drugs.
- Your own prescription drugs in a quantity or manner that deviates from what was prescribed by a licensed physician.
- Your own prescription drugs mixed with something else, especially alcohol.

Just cross these off your list, and I will drill into them specifically. I am going to place the first two bullets above in the same class. Illegal drugs and other people's prescription drugs (which taking others' prescriptions is also illegal, by the way) go in precisely the same category. Both are highly addictive, extremely dangerous, and will change your life for the worse the second you take them. Yes, that sentence is here to scare you, and you should take it seriously. On the straight-up "illegal and we all know it" drugs, you should avoid these entirely. I struggle with providing a list because there are so many and the names change, but you know what I mean; cocaine, heroin, crystal meth, ecstasy, crack, the list goes on.

You will also run across other drugs that sound very scientific like they came directly from the sweet older gentleman who runs the local pharmacy and would never steer you wrong; Fentanyl, Valium, Ketamine, Rohypnol, Ritalin, Oxycodone. Some are legal when prescribed to you by a doctor. Some are not even approved for use country to country due to the dangers. Many of these also have clever names that sound super cool - Special K, Vitamin K, Molly, Fantasy, G-riffic, Cat Valium, and my favorite, Organic Quaalude. I can assure you there is nothing organic about it.

Any of the above mentioned and so many more that float around are incredibly dangerous. You have no control over what someone put in the drugs or used to cut them. Getting you hooked is the primary objective, so you have to have it over and over. The drug dealers generate a nice recurring revenue stream as you destroy your life.

Especially with the more "natural" choices, and we'll dig into this in a minute, you may believe it came from nature, so how bad could it be? Well, although cocaine originates from the coca plant, it passes through many, many hands before it finds its way into that little baggy your friend got from a guy he knows. And in the process, it is mixed with any number of chemicals to aid in smuggling, then reconstituted again with more chemicals. It is then cut with something else white and powdery to make it go farther, and your guess is as good as mine as to what else the drugs may contain. In summary, you don't know what you're taking at all. This is one example, but the same with any illicit drug, and often even with the prescription drugs that find their way onto the street.

There is nothing more upsetting to me than seeing a person who took heroin or cocaine once and can't shake it. And before you even begin to think that you're tough enough that addiction could never happen to you, look around. That's not the case. You are dealing with a chemical reaction designed to circumvent your ability to make decisions, and it does so magnificently. You will not be able to resist it. Therefore, you will become a slave to it. You will lose your money, your family, your friends. They will ultimately distance themselves from you because your decline will be too painful to watch. Those that hang around will do so because they care, but they will also resent you and the pain you create. Relationships will never be the same. I'm not just using dramatic language meant to scare you, it's real life, and I have been through it.

I worked with a guy I considered a pretty good friend back in the mid-90s when crack was the big epidemic. He was a normal guy from a regular middle-class family who was in school and had a good job. We made decent money working as valets at a high-end hotel and left with cash in our pockets every day. I still have no idea why he ever smoked crack the first time but assumed he was hanging with the wrong people who talked him into it. It only took one time to turn him into a raving addict.

Within just a few weeks, he began showing up at work clearly intoxicated, out of his mind. After the second time he almost ran over one of us with a car he was parking, we all got together and told him he needed to stop showing up to work messed up, or we were going to get him fired. When it didn't stop, we went to management and complained, and the company let him go. We all felt terrible about it, this was a friend, but it was putting our safety and the safety of the hotel guests and other workers in jeopardy every time we worked with him.

Within two weeks, he began appearing at the hotel with steaks he had acquired with food stamps. Knowing we had cash in our pockets, he wanted to sell us the steaks for cash so he could buy more drugs. We all agreed not to do it since the money would just allow him to damage himself even more. After a few failed attempts, he stopped coming around entirely. I heard later he had moved back to the mid-west and was biking and healthy. I just learned a few weeks ago he was dead as a result of an overdose.

There is a reason drug addicts and alcoholics never fully recover and are always in "recovery." Once you get pulled in, it becomes your entire life and the lives of everyone around you.

Ok, I hope that all hits home - just don't ever start, and you will not have to deal with recovery and addiction. If you're already in this situation, you know what I am talking about, but please read on because I know it is difficult, but there is hope. We'll get to that in a minute.

Now, we all know that cocaine, heroin, meth, all that crazy, highly addictive stuff is not natural in any way. The next trap is the plant-based stuff, often sourced in your local country or local area — specifically, things like marijuana and mushrooms.

We're getting ready to walk the line here with a changing prescription landscape, so before we get into the plants, I will go back and quickly touch on bullet three above, not abusing your prescriptions. There is, of course, a place for prescription drugs. Pain killers are indeed a miracle of modern medicine when used for the intended purpose of controlling pain. Additionally, prescriptions that can aid with other chronic conditions like depression, anxiety, ADHD are positively life-changing for many people when prescribed and taken correctly under a doctor's supervision. When I say doctor, I mean a reputable physician - not the dude in a lab coat on a billboard, or the hack at the local pain clinic.

The problem with many of these drugs is that they can be as addictive as the illegal stuff even under professional medical guidance. This type of addiction potential is difficult to manage. The best advice I have is that if you find yourself in a situation where you will be taking an addictive prescription, you must inform yourself and understand the dangers. Talk to your doctor and to friends you can trust to watch your back. Never use your prescriptions in doses other than prescribed by a reputable physician. If you ever feel that things are getting out of control, speak up before it's too late.

If you wait too long and the addiction grows, at some point, it will take over, and you will find yourself seeking the same narcotic effects elsewhere, probably in the illegal drugs or other people's prescriptions, as discussed. Avoid that at all costs.

On the same topic, mixing any pill with alcohol presents a risk of death. I'm not going to sugar coat this one since I have lost family members and friends to accidental overdoses when pills and alcohol are mixed. Countless accidental and avoidable celebrity deaths are attributed to these lethal combinations as well. Just Google it, the list is long. The danger is real, and very young and healthy people have made this mistake and ended up in the ground. Again, avoid this at all costs.

Back to the plant-based stuff. This is a slippery slope in expanding on this subject. I don't want to run afoul of the benefits of legitimate natural remedies. In recent years, marijuana has become legal in many U.S. states and many other countries. While the legalities and prescription requirements vary and in many areas are still in question, it has almost bridged the gap into mainstream prescription use for specific ailments. When I was young, the argument for marijuana was, "It's all-natural; how could something that comes straight from nature be bad for you?"

If you want guidance on this, re-read the first part of this chapter. If it comes from a legitimate pharmacy in a dosage prescribed by a licensed, reputable physician, whose motivation is your well-being and not their financial status, use appropriately and understand the risks. If it comes from anywhere else, you are gambling. Marijuana on the street is often mixed with other addictive substances, and you have absolutely no way of knowing what substances or in what quantity.

"But I have this friend named Sunshine, and she lives in the woods and knows exactly which mushrooms to pick off of the cow patties and how to cook them. She's been making mushroom tea for years and knows exactly what to do. It's totally safe".

Here's the problem with taking a "recommended dosage" of any mind-altering substance from someone who uses these particular substances all of the time:

You're taking advice on altering your brain from someone who uses drugs all the time.

Let that marinate for a few minutes and see how it resonates with you. We can move on to the most common drug of all - alcohol. Alcohol is legal, cheap, and readily available. It has commercials on TV...stay thirsty, my friends! How bad can alcohol be? Like anything else, pretty bad if misused.

Those of you who have experienced alcohol and drug addiction first-hand know how bad it can be. Alcohol is highly addictive, without a doubt. If you have an addictive personality to start with, it can take hold quickly. There can be a physical manifestation and also a lifestyle manifestation. Once anything becomes ingrained as a habit and takes hold, the habit can grow. Most of the people I know who ended up in Alcoholics Anonymous (AA) or similar programs and subsequently recovery (and a few who did not make it) started by just meeting friends for drinks after work. Next thing you know, it's every day. Before long, they're the last people in the bar every night, long after the friends have made their way home.

I'm not going to dwell on this. Just be mindful of the dynamic. What I want to focus on with the drinking are a few essential guidelines that, if you follow them, will hopefully keep you safe. I'm not going to vilify drinking wantonly. That would be hypocritical. I drank a little in high school, a little more in college. I also drink today; cocktails on occasion, and I enjoy good beer. I also very much know my limits and abide by the rules below. If you follow these rules, they can help keep things under control to stay safe and healthy.

Don't Ever Operate a Vehicle

I know I don't need to explain this, so we'll move on quickly. In today's climate of ride sharing and ride availability, it is cheap and easy to find a safe ride home. Leave the car where it is. It will be fine. There are only downsides here and zero upsides to drinking and driving. Spend a few bucks on a ride and save yourself a world of problems. The best-case scenario is you drink and drive and make it home safe, only to feel like an asshole the next day for taking an unnecessary risk that you know was wrong. Worst case, you kill someone or yourself, and every other scenario in between these two extremes just plain sucks.

Don't Mix Alcohol with Other Substances

Especially prescription drugs. Mixing drugs and alcohol may be the primary way people overdose. Pop a few Vicodin, have a couple of drinks, fall asleep, and don't wake up. It does not take much to overdose when substances are mixed.

Know Your Limits

It is essential to understand how many drinks you consume and how they affect you over time. Once you begin to feel the effects, it will become increasingly difficult to slow it down and make sound decisions. Know your limits and do not exceed them.

If You Can't Count the Number of Drinks You're Having, You Will End Up in Trouble

This is a simple one. One "drink" is typically;

- 12 oz. of regular American-style lager beer at 4-5% Alcohol by Volume (ABV).
- 8-9 oz. of higher alcohol content beer like IPAs or malt liquor, many times in the 6-9% range, but some go higher.
- 5 oz. of wine which is about 12% ABV
- 1.5 oz. of liquor which is about 40% ABV

On average, and it varies by person, the human body will process out one "drink" in about two hours. So, simple math, if you have more than one drink every 2 hours, you will begin to feel the effects. The faster you drink, the harder it will hit you, and the more impaired you will become.

I'll say it again - if you can't count it, you can't align it with your limits to stay under control.

Here are some examples of how you will lose count and lose control;

- Drinking liquor from the bottle.
- Keg Stands, funnels, or chugging drinks.
- Mixing drinks by just pouring liquor in a glass without measuring.
- Drinking something someone else made and handed to you (more on this critical one below).

Don't Drink Cheap Alcohol

If you are drinking cheap alcohol that tastes like crap - you need to ask yourself why. I'll help - you're doing it for the sole purpose of getting hammered. There you have it; we understand the motives now. So, acknowledge the motive and now take the time to understand your limits and be smart about it. If you're going to drink, drink well. Spend a few more dollars and pick a beer that tastes good, decent wine, or liquor made through a quality process. If you cannot afford to purchase alcohol that you actually like, you probably should be doing something other than going out drinking.

Never Accept an Open Drink from Someone You Don't Know and Trust

And by trust, I do not mean that really cute dude you just met who thinks you are a fabulous conversationalist and has all of the same interests you do. He's magical. Be smart - trust is built over time, a long time. If someone hands you an open drink, first of all, you can't count it, as mentioned above, because you don't know how much alcohol is in it. Second, you don't know what else someone added to it. I will jump specifically to date rape drugs because, as uncomfortable and disturbing as this is, it happens more frequently than anyone would like to think. Someone adds an illicit substance like GHB, Ketamine, or Rohypnol to a drink and hands it to you, with the specific intent of taking advantage of you. These powerful drugs will take hold quickly and render you nearly unconscious and unable to make any type of reasonable judgment. What happens next will not be good in any scenario. Best case, you have friends that can control the situation and keep you safe (see that section below), and you wake up with no recollection of the evening. The list of worst-case scenarios spans the gamut from being robbed to physically violated to killed.

Never Leave Your Drink Unattended

See above, same problems. Leave an open drink where someone else can add something to it, and you are placing yourself in the same potential situation.

You Can't Count on Anyone but Yourself to Keep You Safe

Understand that no matter how responsible your friends are, you have to take responsibility for yourself. You can't count on anyone to make the right decisions for you. Know your limits, be smart, and be safe.

<u>Resources:</u>

SAMHSA's National Helpline is a free, confidential, 24/7, 365-day-a-year treatment referral and information service (in English and Spanish) for individuals and families facing mental and/or substance use disorders. 1-800-487-4889 or <u>https://samhsa.gov/find-treatment</u>

Notes:

TRUST AND RELATIONSHIPS

"The greatness of a man is not in how much wealth he acquires, but in his integrity and his ability to affect those around him positively."

~ Bob Marley

Relationships are the core of everything you do, and the bedrock foundation of solid relationships is trust. Without solid relationships, it isn't easy to go very far in any direction and be successful. Without trust, it is tough to build those relationships.

I have found that it is far better to tell the truth, in all but the most extreme cases, and suffer the consequences of a mistake, rather than mislead or misdirect. This principle holds even when the truth's results could be extreme - getting fired, breaking up, etc. Ultimately, avoiding honesty will come back to bite you. And, you will suffer the guilt of the lie and live in fear of the repercussions until the consequences ultimately come back around.

The positive impact of trust will supersede, or at least offset, the downside of mistakes in most cases.

One of my mentors is a New Orleans lawyer and a businessman. He is a Texan by birth and a New Orleanian because he has been living there for almost 40 years. His New Orleans experience and Texan lineage organically define him as an interesting guy, and his stories alone could generate a book of their own. He is the managing partner of a law firm, and one of his stories provides an excellent example of how trust can make or break a business relationship.

Many years ago, he had a legal secretary whom he really liked. He says that he felt like she could be someone that stayed with him forever, the last legal secretary he would ever hire. He paid her well, she worked hard, and he had every intention of grooming her and keeping her on his staff until he retired. One day it came to his attention that one of his associates was breaking off from the firm and had sent a letter to many of their clients advising of this break and suggesting they follow this associate to his new practice. He also found out that his prized legal secretary had typed and sent the letter. Because the secretary officially worked for both attorneys, it was not entirely unusual for her to have typed and mailed a letter for the associate. The subject matter obviously made handling the letter without disclosing it to the managing partner, at worst, pure mutiny. At best, it was a very questionable decision.

In his direct communication style, he simply asked her about her involvement with the letter. To hear him recount the discussion, he asked her, "On such-and-such a date and such-and-such a time, did you transcribe and send a letter on behalf of [associate attorney] detailing his intent to leave the firm, and then send that letter to some of our clients?". She answered simply, "No."

He describes the sinking feeling of knowing that their relationship was now over, and he was going to lose his most valued employee.

"I'm going to teach you a valuable lesson now, one that will help you in the future, and you'll never forget," he says to her. "If someone ever asks you a question and provides you with that many specifics related to the question, you have to assume they already know the answer to the question they're asking. Now pack your stuff, I have to let you go."

As he recounts the story, she admitted her mistake and begged and pleaded to stay, and you can tell it still bothers him all these years later that he had to let her go. I asked him, "If she was that valuable why didn't you reprimand her and take the time to try to patch the relationship?". He answered simply, "If I can't trust you, I can't work with you". Firing this staff member was not about the initial action that prompted the conversation. It was about the dishonesty when confronted. Had she answered truthfully, I believe his reaction would have still been less than pleasant. Nonetheless, the issue would have passed.

When it comes to trust, the first major tenet is that it must be earned first. Earning trust can take a long time and require many interactions. Being steadfast in honesty over some time is the only way to build genuine, foundational relationships. In a little while, we will get to the money chapter where I tell you that money, for the most part, comes slow and leaves quickly. Trust works the same way. It takes a long time to build trust, and it takes one small, dishonest action to destroy it irreparably. If you make it your mission to act honestly and communicate with integrity, your relationships will form organically.

The second central tenet is that trust is a two-way street, and while you must act in a trustworthy manner, you also have to learn to trust others. Trusting others is difficult for many people, for any variety of reasons. It can be especially difficult for people who have deep-rooted trust issues, based on early childhood development or specific experiences that taught them not to trust. To be a successful partner in trust, you have to be able to place some trust in those you are working with and let them do the heavy lifting to earn the deeper trust.

I am not in any way saying to trust anyone blindly. In the business world, to be an effective leader, you have to be trustworthy, and those you are leading need to work hard to earn your trust. From a leadership standpoint, I have a brilliant friend from Venezuela who always says, "trust but verify." I recently had a situation occur that is relevant to this position. I hired a new member of my management team, a young person who I felt could end up being my right hand in one of my businesses. He was smart, talented, and in my interviews, he checked all of the boxes.

When I hired him, I pulled together a meeting of my management team, and I reiterated to everyone on the team - "I am counting on you guys to manage your areas. I trust you to make good decisions. If you make a mistake, we will work together to correct it and make sure it does not keep happening, but I trust you to do your jobs". Pretty clear.

Within 48 hours, I received my new employee's first report. I read it, it seemed reasonable, and I moved on. I trusted him to give me the honest information I requested. The next day, I had another one of my managers make a comment that contradicted what my new employee had written in the report. I probed this manager, with whom I had already developed a sound relationship and determined that the information my new hire had provided was wrong. It was wrong, but it was also very, explicitly wrong, in a way that seemed designed to mislead me.

Trust but verify.

I decided to give the new employee the benefit of the doubt and asked a very pointed question about his report. I gave him an opportunity to clarify any mistakes. Yet, he gave me a misleading answer that I already knew was not correct. I kept trying to allow him to shoot straight with me. On the third try, he finally admitted that the information provided was only partially true. I politely told him that I was afraid this relationship would not work, and I let him go from the position.

Trust but verify is the right position to take in the early stages of any relationship. At some point, however, the verify part must start to fade into the background. If you are incapable of crossing this gap and have to verify everything all the time, then the other parties in the relationship will quickly grow tired of trying to create a level of trust that may never get there.

There are two primary ways relationships can fall apart due to trust issues;

- When one or both of the parties breaks the trust, or
- When one or both of the parties is incapable of developing the trust in the first place.

Once you have established relationships built upon trust, the world opens up to you in those relationships. Communications get more profound, more honest, and more productive when you trust that the participants come from a place of honesty and good intentions.

<u>Notes:</u>

DATING

"The course of true love did never run smooth."

~ William Shakespeare, "A Midsummer Night's Dream"

Of course, one of the most common relationships where trust plays a role is with your partner, the person you are dating, engaged to, or even married. I want to touch quickly on dating and one-on-one personal, romantic relationships. I will not go into a lot of detail here because, well, I can't. Personal dating relationships are complex. You can't possibly understand what draws people together when you are on the outside.

I have seen so many relationships that I just look at and think, "wow, that'll never work." Yet, years later, the couple is happier than ever, cruising along. I also know couples who seem just to fight all the time, they look miserable to me. But when I ask, they explain that's just how they communicate. They love each other more than anything, and others would not understand. It's true. If you're not in it, you can't understand.

However, there are some things I do understand and some non-negotiable aspects to address. There are times when the head and the heart become conflicted, and you have to be smart enough to see when something is genuinely not working and then make a change.

The first scenario is any type of abuse. The foundation of any real relationship is two-way trust and appreciation of the other person. The moment any type of abuse enters the picture, the trust becomes broken, the appreciation evaporates, and the relationship will not evolve. Physical abuse - of course, is unacceptable in any manner, and if you find yourself in any type of physical altercation with your significant other, end it immediately and get as far away from them as possible, and don't go back. Call the police and file a report and burn the relationship to the ground. It will not improve. People who are predisposed to violence and cannot control their impulses will not change. They will only get more aggressive over time as their level of control over you increases.

Physical abuse is one thing, but mental and emotional abuse can be just as damaging. Many times, they go together. If you feel as though your partner is exerting any mental or emotional control over you, you are not in a relationship that has parity, where both parties are equal. Again, the likelihood is that the longer you allow this go on, the worse it will get. On the flip side, if you are trying to exert control in some way, you need to look inside and evaluate why. If the relationship is worth keeping, you need to assess your motivations and practices and determine if you can correct this. If you cannot, you will end up pushing your partner away.

Next, along the lines with the above, understand that you will not change the other person fundamentally. Small changes and adaptations, sure. I have a ton of habits that my wife really hated going way back — leaving clothes lying around, doors open, not putting dishes in the sink. These things bothered her, so I changed my behavior. She also had quirks that bugged me. I was honest about them, and she changed. If you get on well with someone and respect their feelings, small changes are effortless. I am talking about the big stuff — any ingrained personal trait that can significantly impact your relationship.

Your fiancée just simply can't or won't find a job. He prefers to sit around and watch TV, play video games, and hang out with friends. He takes a small job here or there when you get really adamant about it but can't hold down any position consistently. It bugs you, because you are career-driven and want to grow and develop. Regardless, you just know that you will probably buy a house and even have kids as soon as you are married. The bills will come in, and he will have to get serious about work to help provide for the family. At that point, he will change. *No, he won't - time to move on.*

Your girlfriend goes out and parties three nights a week with her regular friends. It's fun for a while, but as things develop, you have other things you want to do with her on these nights. But this is just what she does and continues to do it, leaving you on your own. Even when work functions or other friend dinners come up, she will go with her regular group first without fail. If you ask her to do otherwise, she gets upset with you and tells you how selfish you are. This trend cannot possibly continue after you are engaged, can it? *It certainly can, and it will.* If it is causing problems when dating, it will likely cause broader issues as the relationship develops. Again, time to move on.

When you realize things are not going to work, there is a business tenet you may hear from time to time in the professional world, "fail fast." Once you realize you have made a mistake and the probability of future success is low, even if it has already cost you a ton of money and time, you need to correct the mistake and direct your energy and resources elsewhere. Otherwise, it will continue to cost more time, more money, more aggravation, and detract from other, more valuable ventures. This dynamic is the same in personal relationships.

Investing in relationships is like investing in a stock. Let's say you purchase a stock for $100. You expect that $100 to grow over time and get better and better - $120, $150...it will continue to develop and grow and be rewarding to you. Yet, over a few weeks, the price drops to $50. Most people are going to hold onto that stock. The feeling is that you lost $50 now, but if you wait long enough, it could go back up, and you might get your original investment back. Even if all of the evidence shows that stock will likely go to $0 and you lose everything, many people will hang in there anyway because just getting to break-even would feel like a win. The more prudent thing to do is to walk away with your $50, accept your losses, and put the remaining $50 to work in something else that you think will grow. Don't hang onto something you know will not work just because of your prior investment in it. Get out of it and move on to something with a higher probability of longer-term, meaningful success.

Breaking up is always hard, but when you realize something is not right, it is much easier in both the short term and the long term to just make the change. In many cases, when a breakup occurs, both parties know it is the right thing to do. In some cases, it comes as a shock. Most of us have been or will be, on both ends of this. Even if you feel like this was your soul mate, and the world is ending - *they weren't, and it's not.* It's over because it wasn't going to work, and the breakup will end up being a positive for you in the longer term. The big thing to remember is that this is a really big world. The next relationship is always right around the corner, and if you do it the right way with the right person, it will be even better than the last.

<u>Notes:</u>

SEX

"Which is recorded of Socrates, that he was able both to abstain from, and to enjoy, those things which many are too weak to abstain from and cannot enjoy without excess. But to be strong enough both to bear the one and to be sober in the other is the mark of a man who has a perfect and invincible soul."

~ Marcus Aurelius, Meditations

Ewwwwww.......uncomfortable. Don't worry, this is not sex education, and it's definitely not tips, tricks, and techniques. No, this is a little more straightforward. Because I am a parent, and the purpose of this book is to keep you on the right path, this will be a mostly pragmatic buzz kill and a lot of "don'ts." I will also address many of the myths and mistruths you may encounter that can lead you into trouble.

The physical act of sex serves primarily to propagate our population. People have sex, babies result, and our species continues to develop and grow. The primary objective of any species is to survive. After food, clothing, and shelter firm up the adults' physical security, they will seek next to make more of their own. Grow the herd, develop strength in numbers, and ensure the survival of the species.

The need for sex is deeply ingrained in us biologically due to thousands of years of development as a species. We must continue to breed to ensure our survival. Therefore, from a physical and mental standpoint, sex has become very appealing because whether we know it or not, our genetics tell us to do it to ensure continued herd survival.

There is a reason sex is appealing and feels good, and that is it. You are programmed by mother nature to want to make babies.

So it is essential to understand the "why" behind the urge to engage in sex so we can understand how to control it and measure the risk versus the reward. As we have discussed, the sole biological purpose for participating in sex is producing babies, so it stands to reason that every time you engage in sex, there is the risk of creating a baby. You may no longer view this as a risk at some point in your life, but right now, I am fairly sure if you are reading this book, you might not want to become a parent yet.

Spoiler alert - a little later in the book, I tell you why you should not get a pet as a young adult because it can negatively impact your lifestyle. You can leave a cat in the house with a litter box and some food and water for a few days while you go to the beach with your friends. You can't do that with a baby. That is a whole different level of cramping your lifestyle.

If you have already become pregnant or a parent, you already know what I mean. Don't be discouraged. Keep reading, and we'll cover that in a few.

I think everyone knows that sex can lead to babies. Of course, I lead right in with babies, which is only a risk in heterosexual sex. It is important in explaining the urges, so it is a natural place to start in the discussion of risk. But nobody of any sexual preference or orientation is immune to the dangers of sexual activity.

The sexually transmitted disease is some scary stuff. I'm not going to get into all of the different indications and details, but we'll hit a few at a high level. There are a few sexually transmitted diseases (STDs) that are a major inconvenience at the very least. These can be pretty painful and embarrassing to discuss with your doctor or parent, but are generally not lethal, treated with traditional medicines, and go away over time. Regardless, you don't want them. Then, you have herpes. This disease comes in many different forms, but it is viral, and there is no permanent treatment. Thus, you are stuck with it for the rest of your life. It will flare up and produce sores that are highly contagious and often visible. You can treat the symptoms, but you can't eliminate it, so you will deal with these flareups forever.

In the late 1980s, HIV, the virus that causes AIDS, came on the scene and, at that time, was viewed basically as a death sentence. For many years, becoming infected with HIV meant a very swift decline. Over the last 30 years, treatments have advanced, and the disease has become more manageable. However, it is a lifetime journey of managing it, and it will ultimately affect your health and relationships.

In recent years, scientists have identified the dangers of HPV, which is also a sexually transmitted virus. This one is contagious but can lay dormant in your system for many years before later, causing issues, potentially up to and including cancer.

Despite babies and diseases, there is this crazy societal fascination with sex. Indeed, entire industries have built up around it, most notably the porn industry. With the availability of basically anything on the internet, sex is all around us, all the time. TV, movies, songs, and porn will have you believe you should be having sex for an hour with strangers three times a week or you're less of a man. Or, you have to be rail-thin and wear slutty clothing to be desirable as a woman.

Let's go back to a statement I made earlier about taking advice and understanding your sources. The porn industry sells the concept of sex as an essential part of your life and then attempts to use sex to separate you from your money. The entertainment industry, in general, glorifies sex as some rite of passage or conquest, or something to be thrown around at parties. Again, consider your sources. Is your favorite rapper, actor, or talk show host qualified to define your values and actions? Casual sex with strangers, or even the very newly acquainted, is a pretty seedy, risky affair for all of the reasons noted here. I hope you will wait to engage in sex until you are ready to make relationship commitments.

For the Boys: Many elements of society will tell you that you are a real man when you are having consistent sex with as many people as possible. Go back and take a read through Chapter 2 and determine who you are trying to impress this way and why. Is taking risks and damaging relationships to put another notch on the bedpost doing anything for you personally? Or, is it just damaging you as well?

For the Girls: Many elements of society will tell you that when you are having consistent sex with as many people as possible, you are a whore. Yep, quite a double standard, but the standard is there. Be very careful what you put out there because what comes back can be an unpleasant reminder of bad decisions. Oh, and don't trust the boys. The less enlightened will try anything to circumvent your morals for their gain.

For everyone: There is a considerable value in developing deep, meaningful relationships that transcend the physical desires ingrained in our evolution. Don't ever start with sex; start with a relationship. Like anything else, there is no rush to jump into actions that present a lot of risk for little reward. Rarely in life can something go wrong because of waiting and considering your options in more detail. If anyone is trying to convince you otherwise and rush into a decision that could negatively affect you, they are doing it to support their agenda, not yours.

So, the risks are on the table and we are aware of the potential consequences. You have weighed the options and decided that, against my advice and the advice of pretty much every other responsible adult everywhere, that a couple of minutes of pleasure is worth the risk. Probably a bad idea, but I'm not going to pretend it doesn't happen, not the point here. So let's kill some myths, provide some guidelines, and try to keep you safe and out of trouble.

Myth #1: Condoms Prevent Pregnancy

No, no, no, and no - condoms do not prevent pregnancy, they *reduce the risk of pregnancy, if used properly*. Many people don't use them properly. Additionally, they can come off, they can break, any number of things can happen to circumvent the protection. Spermicidal lubricants may help, but they are not a panacea and definitely do not provide any guarantees. Go ahead and check the condom box for their guarantee of your safety and future as single person without kids. It's not there, and the condom company will not help pay for medical bills, diapers or day care.

Myth #2: A Girl Cannot Get Pregnant When She Has Her Period

Totally untrue. Menstrual cycles vary greatly from person to person and can even vary month to month. There is a word for people who try to time unprotected sex to avoid pregnancy - "parents".

Myth #3: Oral Sex is Not Really Sex

If you're going down this road, you already know that you're simply trying to justify what you are doing or planning to do. Of course, oral sex is sex. Although pregnancy will probably not result, all of the other stuff listed above is on the table, and this can quickly escalate.

Myth #4: If I Don't Do It S/he Will Leave Me

Ok, not so much a myth, but I will say this; if you are dating someone who threatens to leave you for not having sex, then you should run, not walk, in the other direction. You will not form a relationship based on anything meaningful and are dealing with someone more interested in themself than in you. You will not change this person, especially not by having sex with them.

Myth #5: Impaired Judgement is a One-Way Street

Sex must be a mutual decision in every case, with no exceptions, or it's called rape. No means no, and there is no room for misunderstanding here. In Chapter 5, we covered impaired judgment through drugs and alcohol as one of the risks of becoming sexual abuse victims. By the same token, if your partner is impaired in any way, you risk running afoul of mutual consent. It is critically important that sex involves true, unimpaired, mutual consent with no room for confusion. If there is any room at all for misinterpretation, you cannot even consider proceeding, regardless of what your hormones are screaming at you. Drugs or alcohol will further confuse the situation on both sides, and, especially when engaging in sex with someone for the first time, there cannot be any confusion. If you even think your partner may be in a position in which they cannot form true, informed consent, avoid sex at all costs. If the consent and desire exists on both sides, it will happen in due course, under the right circumstances.

Myth #5: You Can't Get Pregnant in a Pool or Hot Tub, So You Don't Have to Use Condoms

No kidding, I have heard this for years. Totally false. And beyond that, even with a condom it can cause additional issues for the female including urinary tract or other infections, as pools and hot tubs are breeding grounds for bacteria.

Myth #6: It's Not Going to Happen to Me

Any of this is on the table, from STDs to pregnancy, becoming a victim of or being accused of rape. Sex is serious business, and you should treat it as such. Casual encounters can turn into much, much more. As with everything else we discuss here, you have to maintain your faculties, stick to your principles, and make smart decisions based on facts and not emotion.

So, what if it does happen to you? Maybe you are already in one of these situations. You have contracted an STD, been a victim of sexual abuse, or even are pregnant or had a baby. All things that perhaps you would have preferred to avoid, but here we are.

As I said in the introduction, bad times come and go, and so do the good times. Any situation you are in is manageable with the right mentality, support system, and resources, and there is always help available to you. I have listed some resources at the end of this chapter. If you have contracted or suspect you have contracted an STD, please do not wait to see your doctor and take action, and do not pretend it doesn't exist and spread it to others. That is plain wrong and, in most cases, punishable by law. If you have been the victim of sexual abuse, the best thing you can do is talk about it and work to overcome it. It will be very difficult at times, but you must remember you are not alone - far from it. I know many, many people who have been through the exact same things and you are never alone.

Finally, let's talk about babies. Yes, it happens, and it can be scary, especially if you are on your own. If you have become pregnant unexpectedly, I will encourage you, like everything else here, to try to control your emotions, gather information, and make sound decisions. There is a lot to think about, and there are many different paths you can take, most of which end up just fine in the long run for you and the baby. The most important thing is to talk with people you trust about your options and consider the longer-term outlook, not just what is right in front of you.

If you have already had a baby, then hopefully, you have developed a commitment to make the best decisions for that child. That goes for the moms and the dads. Everyone is different, and it always surprises me how many people can create a life and then be totally indifferent to what happens to it. Unfortunately, this is the world in which we live. If you elect to be a responsible parent, it will be hard - sometimes very hard. Honestly, it's the hardest thing I have ever done, and I thought I prepared myself. But, few things in life that are worth doing are easy or comfortable, and it can be the most rewarding thing you ever do to see your child grow and succeed. I know many single moms and dads who were also unprepared to have children, and it was very, very hard at first, but it always ended up working out. Whatever you do, try to make the right decisions for you and the child, and don't give up.

Resources:

National Domestic Violence Hotline (https://www.thehotline.org) or 1-800799-7233 is staffed with advocates available 24/7/365 to talk confidentially with anyone experiencing domestic violence, seeking resources or information, or questioning unhealthy aspects of their relationship.

RAINN is the National Sexual Assault Telephone Hotline. Calling 800-656-4673 will connect you with a trained staff member from a sexual assault service provider in your area. They route calls based upon the first six digits of your phone number or your zip code, and do not store your information.

<u>Notes:</u>

58

TOBACCO

*"We do realize that today's teenager is
tomorrow's potential regular customer."*

~ Philip Morris Memo, 1981

Please just don't start. There is no reason for using tobacco
at all in any form. We know it's carcinogenic, can cause
cancer. We know that smoking and vaping can do horrible
things to your lungs. It is highly addictive, super expensive, and
prices and taxes are only going up. Big waste of money that you
could put to use elsewhere.

I can think of only one reason anyone starts using tobacco
products; they somehow think it makes them look cool. It doesn't.
You're not a 1950's movie star, and by the way, many of them died
early from lung cancer. Farthest thing from cool, just don't start.

If you've already started, the list of reasons to stop is long. I
understand how difficult this can be, having done it myself. Again,

this is not some "holier-than-thou" rant. I started using smokeless tobacco in college. Just a bad decision I made one day that turned into a habit I could not break, that lasted ten years. I realize now just how silly it was, and that likely most people thought I was just foolish, which, of course, I was. It took me ten full years to free myself of the hold that smokeless tobacco had on me. Ten years of moral dilemma and aggravation, knowing I had made a poor decision, but not being able to shake the addiction, even though I understood the immediate and longer-term dangers.

Tobacco is highly addictive physically, to begin with, some say on the level of opiates. But there is also a lifestyle hook. You may start associating the use of tobacco products with activities, such as going out with friends or getting home from work and relaxing. The reality is, the relaxing effect of tobacco is temporary, and it actually does more to create stress in your system, leading you to need more to get back to relaxing.

Sounds a heck of a lot like describing the drugs in Chapter 5, doesn't it?

If you're hooked and trying to quit, you need to break both the physical and the mental associations with tobacco use. There are many ways to go about this, and there are free programs available to help you. I have listed some resources at the end of the chapter. There are also some basic steps you can take to try to transform on your own. The important thing is not to get discouraged. Understand that some people can just quit cold turkey, but most will have to try 5,10,15 times before it sticks.

You don't want to get to the point where it takes a health scare to make you quit.

It can take two weeks or more to break the physical connection and be an even longer, more challenging process to break the mental associations.

Remove Access

Make it difficult to get to the tobacco product. If it is sitting on the counter, your temptation is right in front of you.

Break the Connection

Remove the factors that trigger your desire to use. Stop going out for a few weeks or start exercising after work rather than sitting down with a smoke. You must break all associations.

Get Accountable

Negative reinforcement is often much more potent than positive reinforcement when trying to do something difficult. Get a friend who is willing and able to hold you accountable. Set up a penalty. Every time you smoke or dip, it costs you $10 that you will donate to charity. Be honest, and let your friend hold your money. Nobody wants to lose money, and this can be a powerful motivator for sticking to your goals.

The physical addiction will break only over time. Take the steps above and just hunker down. After two weeks, the urges will start to wane, and within a month, you will be free. Then don't go back - don't get lulled into the false sense of security that you stopped once and you can do it again. It was hard the first time and will be hard, or even harder, the second time. It is essential to understand your initial accomplishment and not slip backward.

<u>Resources:</u>

The Truth Initiative (<u>https://truthinitiative.org</u>) provides research and resources, facts and analysis on issues surrounding tobacco and even some other substance abuse. Just reading the information and document disclosures on how these large corporations try to manipulate people, especially young people, will definitely make you angry enough to prevent you from starting. It might even give you the motivation to quit if you are already hooked.

Notes:

STRESS

*"The greatest weapon against stress is our
ability to choose one thought over
another."*

~ William James

Stress management is a crucial facet of maintaining general health and well-being. While some stress can be a good thing, prolonged or irrational stress should be controlled at all costs. Undergoing extreme stressors for extended periods can contribute to both mental and physical health problems.

I learned a lot about controlling emotions and thinking critically in crises during my time working with Emergency Medical Services. I worked for some time in New Orleans as an Emergency Medical Technician (EMT). This work was rewarding but also dangerous and stressful. We dealt with all types of medical emergencies and trauma situations with people of all ages. One of the things you learn quickly is that almost everyone you encounter in this job counts on you, many for their very survival. If you come unglued and cannot think clearly, it can cost lives. You have to process information quickly and, no matter how difficult the situation, control emotions, and make rational decisions based upon facts. Those stressful situations were challenging and very real and provided a substantial level of training.

This skill set has served me well, thinking clearly during emergencies or even just critical discussions. However, I am personally predisposed to being kind of Type-A, or stressful, personality. This trait has often presented problems in that while I appear very cool on the outside, I am literally coming apart on the inside. Very unhealthy, and I have experienced physical problems as a result of extreme stress. Some of these stresses are real, and some result from just mental junk - thoughts about things that could happen, could have happened, conversations I may or may not even have, and general negative thoughts.

The quote at the beginning of the chapter is true. We have the option to think about things in any way we want. Framing your thoughts is a powerful skillset if you can understand it and master it. When you encounter a very stressful situation, the first question is; Is this stress real or perceived?

If the stress is simply perceived or even made up, it should be fairly straightforward to address. Think about the realities behind the situation and the alternatives. *I am getting on a plane to go on vacation; what if the plane crashes and I die and don't get to my vacation?* The reality is, statistically, commercial air travel is one of the safest modes of transportation. Furthermore, what happens in the more likely scenario that the plane doesn't crash? You'll get to see someplace new and have a great time on vacation. How awesome is that? It does not make any sense to stress over an improbable negative, rather than spending your mental energy planning for the more likely positives.

If the stress is perceived, you can simply reframe your thinking and control it in many cases. If the stress is real, on the other hand, address it with real action. I have a few personal examples from my earlier days in management.

In the first example, I had to have a tough conversation with an employee. It was a conversation that, I was fairly sure, would end up with that person either quitting or my firing them. At a minimum, it was going to be a stressful, heated discussion. I found myself spending huge amounts of time playing the scenarios over and over in my head. In some scenarios, I was confrontational; in others, more passive. In every scenario, the anticipation of the conversation was just plain stressing me out. My challenge was not really in having the conversation - it was the anticipation of the conversation. The actual alternatives were either have it or not have it. If I don't have the conversation, I will continue to worry about it knowing that it eventually needs to happen. Simultaneously, the problems we need to discuss will only worsen and create more stress — the ultimate downward spiral. There is only one solution - do it.

We talked and, in the end, we hit the issue head-on, had a great conversation, and corrected the problems. The actual discussion was not stressful at all. The made-up anticipation of the conversation had created the stress. The Roman philosopher Seneca correctly stated, "We suffer more in imagination than in reality." The resolution to my angst was reframing and controlling my thoughts and taking action.

Example number two, I had taken on a very large project. I do mean very large, almost too large for me, I thought, and I was not sure at all how to start. I spent days considering the enormity of this project, doubting my ability to get it done, and playing out all of the scenarios that would occur when I ultimately failed. This dynamic created an enormous amount of stress, doubt, uncertainty, and even more stress. The solution to this real but addressable pressure was to do something. Do anything. I had thus far done nothing and therefore had no reason at all to doubt my abilities or draw negative conclusions. There is a saying from a Chinese proverb that loosely translates as "A journey of a thousand miles begins with a single step." So, I did something.

I made a list of the first five things I had to do. Just five things. I did not try to fully understand every element of the project or develop a monstrous project plan. I took on the first of the five tasks, then the second, and found that not only did the results come easily, but I felt good about the progress and gained a deeper understanding of how to handle the next phase of the project. Taking even a small action in a huge project allowed me to reduce the stress and make the progress I needed.

Finally, I will touch on job stress, and I will cover this more in-depth in the work chapter. I worked for a really, really awful group of people at one point. They created a work environment that was not just stressful but would be considered abusive in most circles. I was young, did not know much better, and was in a situation where I was kind of trapped. At least I felt trapped. The job stress, combined with the feelings of almost imprisonment, created this overwhelming anxiety in just showing up every day. The only way to alleviate this was to make a change, but that would be hard, which caused even more stress.

So, I finally sat down and literally made a plan. I wrote down a list of jobs I wanted and for which I felt qualified. I made a list of decision-makers to contact and updated my resume to be more enticing to my identified targets. I spent just a little time every day doing something, anything, toward my goal of finding a new job. I was not free, by any means, but just having the direction was a tremendous relief. Making even a little bit of steady progress every day toward my goals also helped me redirect my focus from the negative of the present to the future's positive possibilities. In many cases, the best way to confront stress head-on is to take action.

<u>Notes:</u>

RELIGION AND SPIRITUALITY

"I used to pray that God would feed the hungry, or do this or that, but now I pray that he will guide me to do whatever I'm supposed to do, what I can do. I used to pray for answers, but now I'm praying for strength. I used to believe that prayer changes things, but now I know that prayer changes us, and we change things."

~ Mother Teresa

This is not about organized religion, per se, but more about some considerations concerning studying spirituality and religion and finding your path. I have found a lot of peace in different philosophies and spiritual practices. Especially when dealing with overwhelming stress, some level of mindfulness, and a more in-depth understanding of your inner workings can sometimes help you map a path out of a bad situation. I'm going to talk Christian stuff here for a minute, but only to set the context for this chapter's discussion points. Again, I will not discuss the virtues or drawbacks related to any particular religion. Instead, I shall describe in more general terms the religious and spiritual considerations encountered through my journey.

I grew up predominantly in a Protestant Christian church. My family went to church most Sundays, and we learned about the Old Testament and the New Testament of the Christian Bible. If you are not familiar, the Old Testament is also the basis of Judaism. In the Christian faith, with respect to the New Testament, it is believed that Jesus of Nazareth was born to the Virgin Mary as the Son of God and that his teachings are God's actual word. To oversimplify the full story as recounted in the New Testament, the Romans execute Jesus, and three days later, he rose from the dead and now sits in heaven with God. It is believed that he died for the sins of humans, and to achieve eternal life with Jesus, you simply have to acknowledge and believe in him as the Son of God.

In general, the story of Jesus Christ is beautiful from the beginning to even the violent end. The stories recounted in the New Testament of the Christian Bible, as in many other great religious texts, contain messages of peace, love, and acceptance; treating people as you would want to be treated, standing up for the oppressed, and sacrificing parts of yourself in some way in service of those in need. There is no way to argue that when you live this type of life, supporting and helping others and accepting people of all different types, the positive energy will return to you.

The challenge I always had was with the end of the story. According to most, if not all sects of the Christian faith, if you do not accept Christ as your savior, you will pretty much suffer in hell for eternity after you die. No chance of getting to heaven and being reunited with the rest of us Christians. As a kid, this bothered me. I have always been fortunate to have a lot of friends of different faiths, and the fact that they would not be able to hang out with me for eternity because of their belief system was troublesome. There were my Jewish friends, Muslim friends, and even the atheists. Was I just lucky? I happened to be born into a family that already had an inside track to eternal heavenly bliss by being on the right side of understanding and acknowledging God. But, what about my friends with other belief systems? They are good people, too. Could a truly loving God turn their back on a child born to a family that taught them something different - and send them to hell when they die without even giving them a chance? This premise did not reconcile for me at all. What about the kid born in a remote village in India, who was only ever exposed to Hinduism and never even knew about Jesus?

The point of all of this is not to say that the story of Jesus is right or wrong. The point is to say that it is ok to question and analyze and come to conclusions that make sense and feel right. I have found my place of reconciliation with all of this and come to a personal understanding of what I believe. That was done by reading and studying many religious texts and understanding some different spiritual practices and the primary tenets of other faiths.

It will serve you well to research, read, and experience when it comes to religion and spiritual practice. Locking on to the first thing you were ever introduced to and outwardly rejecting everything else is a very close-minded approach. If you dig into the details, the larger world religions are very similar in many ways. The God(s) are different, as are the spiritual practices, but many of the messages are the same. Seek to understand the entire picture, and you may end up understanding yourself in the process.

At the same time, you may decide that a particular religion is correct, right for you, and this is where you want to commit your time to learn, understand, and practice. That is great.

Faith can be an awesome thing - having the ability to believe in something you cannot see or prove but that you feel in your soul is right. I sometimes envy people I meet who have a level of faith that I just can't seem to achieve. True faith based on research and an underlying belief system can be powerful. Blind faith, or believing things just because someone told you so, is incredibly dangerous. Do the heavy lifting and find your path through reading and research, not taking the first easy path you encounter.

Notes:

ORGANIZATIONS AND MEMBERSHIPS

*"I don't want to belong to any club that
will accept me as a member."*

~ Groucho Marx

There are people in all phases of life who will try to take advantage of you. It is a sad fact, but it is true. The proverbial wolf in sheep's clothing is always lurking, but sometimes these people are hiding in plain sight. And they are just waiting to take you for a ride, figuratively or literally.

Organizations and groups were all formed for a reason, and often that reason is noble. Some may have started as a noble cause and then perverted over time, and others began for nefarious reasons.

I am in no way devaluing the relationships that can form or the personal and professional merits of a group membership. I am simply warning you to evaluate any organization or association carefully, before committing your time, money, resources or emotions. I have personally benefitted from group membership and built some solid relationships as a result. I have also been taken for money and felt like a fool for chasing a group association.

This type of thing typically happened when I needed something badly. It happened when there was something that I needed personally, whether emotional or financial, and someone identified that need and exploited it. The primary way people are pulled in and taken advantage of is the spoken or unspoken promise of addressing a fundamental need.

Are you trying to find yourself? Find religion or spiritual peace? Make more money? Get a new job? Join a family environment that you never had before? All noble quests and all open you up to exploitation if you are not careful. Organizations that promise these things, then turn them around on you for their own benefit, exist in all phases of life from religious and spiritual groups to street gangs.

If you have already been taken advantage of by a group association, unless you are dealing with a criminal act and there is some legal avenue you can pursue, simply try to get over it and move on. There is no sense dwelling on it - some brilliant people have been pulled into organizations and scammed, swindled, or worse. You may have lost some money or some dignity, or even just feel ashamed for being duped. But it happens every day to a lot of people.

Most people you will encounter have the best intentions in mind. You may be at a place in life where you feel lost and need guidance or are confused about your spirituality, sexuality, life direction, or any particular problem that is difficult to discuss.

When the opportunity to fill a personal need shows up in the form of a group or organization that understands your issues and wants you to be involved, it merits assessment. However, don't run headlong into the first potential solution you find. Assess the group closely, look at their structure, look at the motivations, evaluate what drives them. Ask around. See if anyone knows others who have been in the organization or left the organization and speak with them. Do your research before making any type of commitments, especially emotional and financial commitments.

Beyond not jumping directly into the first thing you find, you also have to be very wary of a group when certain factors are present and certain red flags arise. Here are some key elements to watch.

An All-Powerful Leader

Perhaps there is a mysterious man or woman who the group, as a whole, believes has all of the answers and is in firm control of the organization. This person could be billed as a financial prodigy, a prophet, or even a "genius" who drives the mentality and the actions of the group. When there is a power structure that goes back to a single, all-powerful person or even governing entity whose decisions you are not permitted to question, you may have a hierarchy of servitude. In this scenario, others are placed above you, which is a slippery slope into being controlled.

Additionally, in this type of structure, the other group members probably feel the same way about this leader and will think and act on the instruction of one person, one small group, or one doctrine. This structure presents a dangerous opportunity for pure groupthink to take hold. A next iteration is a group acting purely on instruction and not through assessing options and thinking as individuals.

Urgency to Join

Act now, or you will certainly lose your spot. Any time someone uses pressure tactics in a situation, you should be very wary of why. Creating a sense of urgency to jump into a commitment is a tactic that some use to prevent individuals from carefully evaluating the facts of the situation. Usually, the person applying the pressure is hiding something, and it is time to take a step back and assess the situation in more detail.

High Price of Admission

I am sure many organizations are worth a financial investment. Some have legitimate cost structures to support, where donations or dues are necessary to maintain buildings, develop materials, do charity work, provide research, etc. Ensure that admission cost does not strictly serve to tie you to the group, with little to no personal return. That is, where you feel like your investment will make you have to stay to get your money's worth. Next, don't spend money you do not have or with which you cannot afford to part. If an organization is willing to let you max out your credit card to join, they are just another business trying to make a buck and do not have your best interests in mind.

Acts of Commitment

Watch out for any requirements designed to tie you permanently to the group and remove pieces of your individuality. You have to do this particular thing that everyone else has done to show your loyalty. Acts of commitment are a gigantic flag, especially when the action goes against your belief system. Every time you do something for the group that violates what you believe in - a little piece of yourself leaves, and a little piece of the group takes its place. This is how cults are formed, through acts of commitment that pull you in, to a degree you cannot escape.

Attempts to Use your Best Qualities Against You

"We know you are a very loyal person, so we want you to do this deed to show your loyalty." Or, "We know how committed you are, so you should sign this paper showing your commitment agreeing to pay a penalty if you leave." Which you would never do anyway because you are a committed person, right?

Disclosure of Sensitive Information

In line with the above, "we know how honest you are, so we want you to tell us your darkest secrets and show your honesty." Taking sensitive information to use against you later is a common cult tactic. One big caveat here is legitimate psychological therapy or participation in board-certified therapy groups, where disclosing private or sensitive information is a legitimate part of the healing process. Here, I am talking about where a private, non-clinical group wants you to disclose intimate facts about yourself for the stated purpose of being a "better member" or a "more committed" part of the group. The likelihood here is that the information will be kept and used against you later should you try to leave. This tactic is one more advanced organizations use to try to ensure you can never leave. If you leave or stop paying dues or try to discuss the group's work with anyone outside, your private information would be released, causing embarrassment or humiliation.

Individual Motivations

Look at who benefits from your presence in the group and how. Assess the motivations of the group and assess who is gaining from your presence, and what they stand to gain. In a truly supportive organization, you should gain as much as anyone else. When you feel like everyone will advance except you, or that you will have to do an excessive amount of work or achieve some preordained levels to realize a personal reward, be very careful.

Group and organization associations can be quite beneficial, but always watch out for the signs that the group or leader motivations are centered more around their benefit than your own. When you ultimately do your due diligence and decide to join an organization, always remember to maintain your autonomy. Never lose sight of yourself as an individual or compromise yourself for the will or benefit of others. If you fall into or have already fallen into these traps, remember there is always a way out. It may burn down the relationships and may even cause some emotional or financial strain or embarrassment. If you are involved with an organization that is not working for you but against you, it is time to part with the prior investment and move on, as with any other relationship.

<u>Notes:</u>

DIVERSITY

*"We all should know that diversity makes
for a rich tapestry, and we must
understand that all the threads of the
tapestry are equal in value no matter what
their color."*

~ Maya Angelou

I cannot stress enough the value of building relationships and gaining an understanding of as many ethnicities and belief systems as possible. Much of the way people operate, as it goes to interacting with others, is driven by early childhood and young adult experiences. I was fortunate to have grown up in a household where there was no discrimination or pressure to avoid or persecute people based upon their skin color or sexual preferences, or anything else. Additionally, I went through school with a vast array of people, and we were kind of just friends with everyone. At least, if we weren't friends, it was not related to any of the factors listed above.

Regardless of how you were raised, it is never too late to learn to appreciate everyone and gain from different perspectives and life experiences. When you cross the bounds of race or ethnicity, there is a lot to learn on the other side. Discrimination or fear of different groups defines learned behavior, and it can be unlearned. It may seem uncomfortable, and you may not even like some of it, but there is no harm in seeking understanding. In fact, I would say it is incumbent upon you to gain a full life experience on this planet as a human being, to branch out of your comfort zone, and experience new ideas and new types of people.

There is a whole, wide world out there of different people with different upbringing, life experiences, foods, cultures, and traditions. You should try to experience as many of them as possible. Not only can it be rewarding, but it's also pretty fun.

You don't even have to travel or spend money to branch out. As you make friends that cross these lines, you will find that people are more than willing to share their experiences with you. Eat a new food at someone's house, go to a different religious service, or attend local ethnic music or cultural events in your town. All of these options are typically free and available to you, should you choose to experience what is out there beyond your walls.

<u>Notes:</u>

TATTOOS

*"The world is divided into two kinds of
people: those who have tattoos, and those
who are afraid of people with tattoos."*

~ Unknown

You might assume here comes the old guy who has no tattoos telling you what you should or, more likely, should not do with your body. Not so, in fact, far from it. The quote above I just put in because I find it humorous. Illustrative, possibly accurate in many circles, but really just kind of funny.

I am only using the tattoo as a representative example of the importance of taking the time to reason through decisions that could impact you in the future. The tattoo, as a semi-permanent, if not permanent, decision seems to fit the bill.

Additionally, it is one of those decisions often born of emotion and acted upon in haste (and many times under the influence). It is also a decision that is often regretted later in life. So much to work with here - but only a few quick items of note to consider.

First, many people get tattoos to commemorate something they want to remember. As life goes on, the problem is that sometimes things you want to remember later become things you want to forget. Permanent reminders sometimes work in unintended ways.

Next, your overall lifestyle will likely change dramatically as you get older, and you never know where this will take you. I only have one small story regarding a friend who got a tattoo in college. She had a few drinks in her, was convinced to go along with a friend to the tattoo parlor, and ended up with a body decoration of her own. It was a common symbol of no particular personal meaning, placed in an inconspicuous location. Her idea with the placement was that this would not cause a problem in later professional settings - until it did. At that time in college, she had no idea that her professional career would take her to a sub-tropical location, where the primary executive activity was beach volleyball. Oops - and she had this silly looking tattoo that, when wearing beach gear, was all of a sudden displayed prominently, despite her "planning."

Now, maybe she could have explained a well thought out or artistic, deeply personal display. However, she could only describe this symbol as a drunken mistake, and a modestly embarrassing one, at that. The process to remove the tattoo required 6 painful visits and cost roughly 10 times what it cost to have the tattoo done in the first place. My friend told me later that every single removal visit was far worse than getting the tattoo applied.

Again, I am not against the art of the tattoo in any way. But it is an easy example of the importance of thinking through the potential longer-term impact of decisions that could affect you for many years, if not your entire life.

Notes:

PETS

I remember a sign on the door of the building I lived in during college that stated no pets permitted unless they could breathe underwater for 24 hours. I also recall several people who actually had fish in their dorm rooms, presumably just because they could - which is a bad reason to do most things.

What you have to remember about pets is that they are a giant responsibility. When you take on that responsibility, you are taking on another life that will depend on you for everything - food, water, cleanliness, medical care, even where and when to go to the bathroom in many cases. These things cost money and require time and attention. So many people take on pets with no idea how to care for them or what to expect. Ultimately, this ends up in a situation where the pet is uncared for, given away, or worse, sent to a shelter.

This subject reminds me of the Steven Covey principle, "Begin with the end in mind." When you start a project, any project, don't look at just today but begin to explore the outer years and where you think this project is going. In the case of pets, you're dealing with an impact on two lives, theirs and yours. Most animals that people take in as pets live for quite a long time if cared for properly - easily over ten years, and in some cases much, much longer.

I certainly value the time spent with my pets. I took some in via adoption, some in by accident. Picked up one in particular that someone had thrown out, who was like a child to me. Animals can definitely add a wonderful dimension to the right home or environment. I encourage adoption or otherwise taking in an animal that will fit your lifestyle and theirs.

Most people make a mistake, especially young people, of taking on too much, too soon, with unrealistic expectations, and failing to realize the impact a pet will have on their lifestyle. My advice to any young person who has not yet entered the professional world is to wait until your life stabilizes until taking on a pet - any pet. By stabilize, I mean you are in the working world with a steady income and living situation appropriate for that animal. If you are in a school of any kind, don't even think about it. Pets take giant amounts of time and cost money to care for properly. Additionally, make sure you have a life plan or outlook that supports that animal's continued care.

Even the ones who can breathe underwater for 24 hours require fairly consistent care. Fish seem easy - put them in a bowl or tank and drop in a little food every couple of days. Not really the case. Anyone who has ever cleaned a fish tank can attest that it is a giant hassle. The process alone can jeopardize the fish's safety in transferring them between containers and stabilizing water temperatures and pH. It is difficult, requires equipment, and has a cost - but it must be done regularly to ensure their well-being.

Birds, turtles, hermit crabs, reptiles - all require the same care.

When you get to dogs and cats, the time commitment goes to the next level. They require a lot of personal attention, in addition to cleaning and feeding. Many people take on these animals because they are cute and have personality and people just "want them." Making a sensible decision based on facts is where the planning comes in. When you consider dogs and cats, the most common and available pets, you're probably looking at $1500 per year minimum to support each one. This number can be more if you plan on doing any travel or your work commitments require long hours, and you have to pay for additional care.

If you are a young student or professional just entering the working world and can afford this, that is the first consideration. The next consideration is where you will be in the next 5, 10, or 15 years you have this pet. Are you thinking about doing a lot of traveling? You will have to find and pay someone who can care for your pet. If you think you might move to a different country for a while - most likely cannot take them with you without an expensive and lengthy process to get them cleared for transit. Many apartments and rental houses will not allow pets or will require larger security deposits. They will also typically have stringent requirements, so you will significantly restrict where you can live every time you search for a new place. If you are thinking about moving to a different locale, like from a rural setting to a large city, will this move allow you to support the pet? Or, if you plan on marrying and having children, will the pet fit into this lifestyle?

Pets are fantastic when you have the means and the lifestyle to support them. When you don't, they turn into major stress and distraction very quickly. My point to all of this is simple, don't make decisions in haste that will negatively impact your life and the life of an animal. Wait until you have the means, the lifestyle, and the forward-looking plan before deciding to take on the responsibility of another life that will count on you for literally everything.

<u>Notes:</u>

DIET AND EXERCISE

"Eat less and move around more."

~ Walton and Johnson

Long-time U.S. radio personalities John Walton and Steve Johnson espoused the principle of "eat less and move around more" as the solution to obesity. Generally speaking, if you have to adopt a simple plan for weight loss or weight control, it's a pretty good place to start. While the principle is sound, and the phrase has somehow stuck with me for many years, the reality is the subject of diet and exercise is just a little more complicated than that.

Many countries worldwide are experiencing a significant rise in obesity, especially in younger generations. Obesity is a health crisis that threatens to put a massive strain on healthcare systems but, more importantly, leads to health conditions like diabetes and heart disease, and ultimately the early death of younger and younger folks. These conditions are mostly avoidable. While I do not represent this as medical advice, I will present some simple guidelines by which I try to live. These guidelines are based on simple principles and may shed some light on your personal situation, especially if you struggle with health and weight issues.

It may sound cliche, but your body is an engine, and the food and drink you put into it is the fuel that drives that engine and keeps it clean. Just like putting cheap, old, dirty gas in your car will ultimately destroy the engine, putting cheap food filled with chemicals and sugar will eventually hurt your engine.

In my opinion, a poor diet is the root of many health issues today. In my mid to late twenties, I had put on quite a bit of weight. Not sure if I qualified technically as "obese," but I was probably knocking on the door. My cholesterol was too high, and I was just generally not very fit. My lack of fitness was confusing, given that I worked out at the gym almost every day during lunch. I worked in the yard all weekend and spent lots of time outdoors, engaged in some measure of physical activity. I was doing what I thought were all the right things, but the weight was not coming off. I had a lot of muscle but was also carrying a lot of gut.

It was not until I began to address my diet effectively that I could bring things into check. I would finish my lunchtime workout and then grab a wrap on the way back to the office. The wrap was a healthy lunch from my perspective at that time. In retrospect, processed meats, cheese, and creamy sauces on a grain wrap filled with sugar and some fried chips on the side kind of checks many of the boxes of things you want to avoid. And they were all together right there in my "healthy" lunch. I was unaware that, through my diet, I was basically negating everything I was doing in the gym.

There are certain areas of life in which the phrase "everything is ok in moderation" is applicable, and I believe diet is one area.

The keys are balance and understanding. First, you have to understand what is actually good and bad. Then, take in enough of the good stuff and limit the bad stuff. Here are some considerations.

Processed Foods, Sugar and Salt

Processed food is everywhere and is usually cheap and easily accessible, which makes it quick for grab-and-go or if you are on a tight budget, but the health impacts can be drastic. Processed food traditionally contains a significant amount of sugar, salt, and preservatives. Keep any of the items in this category in tight check, and don't let them become major parts of your diet. Anything in a can, fried, many frozen foods, cooked and packaged meats and snack foods will qualify.

Fast Foods

You should simply avoid most fast food. Heavily processed meats and fried foods are the hallmarks of traditional fast food. The frying process for cooking is cheap, fast, and easy - profitable for restaurants but a disaster for your health. One thing to watch out for is items billed as "healthy" fast food. Where processed meats and sugary bread are involved, it may not be as healthy as you think.

Fruits and Vegetables

Eat as many as you can. That's all there is to it. There is no down-side to fresh fruits and vegetables. They are typically, pound for pound, much less expensive than meats or snack foods, and they have the health benefits with little preparation.

The biggest thing to look out for here is salad. Sounds strange, I know, but salads can contain a giant amount of sugar and fat because of the dressings and toppings. Just because it is called a salad does not make it healthy. Pay attention to the ingredients.

Light and Low-Fat Foods

When you eat whole, pure foods, you generally don't have to worry about light or heavy, fat or non-fat. These are devices that food companies invented to control their markets. The reality is, if you take away one thing from a product that makes it taste good, you have to add something else to make it taste just as good. Remove the sugar and replace it with artificial sweetener, and now it is "light." Or, pull out the fat and replace the fat with more sugar, and now it is "low fat." Review the ingredients of the things you eat and just be informed, rather than taking label information at face value that it is "good for you."

Food Sensitivities

This is a bit of a sidebar, but perhaps important to know when breaking down food into the categories above. Many people have sensitivities to certain types of food. The most common are lactose from dairy and gluten from wheat products. Soy can also cause discomfort for some people who cannot process it easily. If you find that you experience intestinal discomfort after certain meals or other symptoms such as diarrhea or nausea, consult with your doctor. You may simply be sensitive to something you are regularly eating. Many people suffer with intestinal problems for years, only to find out they were sensitive to something. If you are experiencing similar symptoms, speak with your physician, who can give you some guidance.

All in all, these things should not scare you, just taken as information that you should be aware of. I want you to be mindful of the traps so you can avoid them and maintain a balanced lifestyle. I still eat a burger from time to time - just had fries at a restaurant last week, coated in ketchup and mayo and they were fantastic. You just can't do it all of the time. Understand the traps and balance healthy and unhealthy elements. And, trust me, when you only eat fries on occasion, they taste a lot better.

Hydration

Proper hydration is incredibly important to overall health and well-being. You could probably survive for many days in the wilderness without food. You most certainly would not survive long without water, which is critical for maintaining a healthy physiological balance. Dehydration is widespread among teenagers and young adults. It can cause any number of physical effects from muscle fatigue to bad breath to just general fogginess or lack of mental acuity. Drinking plenty of water can help avoid these problems and help you maintain a feeling of fullness, preventing the craving for unhealthy snacks between meals that leads to weight gain. Often thirst can be mistaken for hunger so, if you're hungry - maybe have a glass of water first.

Many other factors can contribute to the need for more water than your baseline. If you are exercising and losing fluids or simply living in a hot and humid environment, you may require more fluids. You are likely hydrated when you do not feel constant thirst, and your urine is clear or light yellow. A common concept is that the proper amount of water to drink is eight 8-fluid ounce glasses of water per day. This measure is a fine guideline, and provides a good starting point, but the short answer is to listen to your body and drink when you are thirsty. If you need help to determine what is right for you, a doctor can assist with the process.

Exercise

There is a physics principle, Newton's first law of motion, that states a body in motion tends to stay in motion, and a body at rest tends to stay at rest. Even though this statement is related to physics, I have found it applicable to exercise habits. People who develop a healthy and enjoyable habit of exercise will tend to keep doing it. Those who develop a habit of sitting around doing nothing will continue down that road.

Some level of moderate physical exercise will contribute significantly to your overall health and well-being. Besides the physical benefits, even light exercise can help get you in motion and clear your head. The problems of the day seem to fade away when you have time to get outside, sweat and little, and reset your mind.

I have to state the obvious here that you should consult a physician before beginning any exercise regimen, and always start slow and listen to your body. When getting into exercise, there are a few things to consider.

Exercise Doesn't Have to be Expensive

There are plenty of people in this world who would love to separate you from your money, and a lot of money changes hands in the diet and exercise space. You do not require expensive equipment, gym memberships, or subscriptions to get an adequate amount of exercise. Walking is one of the best forms of exercise, and it is low impact and essentially free. I heard an interview once with Mike Tyson that he was walking up to 60 miles per day at the height of his championship boxing training, similar to how the

Spartans trained in ancient times. Even a modest 30 minutes of walking a day can provide the benefits of increased cardiovascular performance and calorie burn.

At the next level, running is also essentially free and requires only a pair of shoes to get started. Running is more taxing on the body, and it is important that you warm up properly and start slow. You should not set out trying to run 2 miles on day one. There are plenty of resources for couch-to-5K type programs that show you how to start slow and work your way up.

If you are interested in building muscle mass or toning muscles, body-weight exercise is just as effective as pushing dumbbells around in a gym. Pushups, free squats, crunches, pull-ups, dips - these can all be done quite easily with either no additional equipment or equipment found commonly around the house or at a park or playground.

Find Exercise that You Enjoy

The biggest challenge to keeping your body in motion is to do what you like. Since I was a kid, I have been on bikes, and I really enjoy getting outside on a bike. The exercise benefits were there, but riding a bike never really felt like work, and I always felt great when finished. If exercise is fun, you will stick with it.

Know Your Limits and Do What Feels Right

You don't have to bench 200 pounds or run marathons, and if you're trying to impress someone else, you will get hurt. Take all exercise advice (including this) for what it is and consider it, but ultimately you must listen to your own body.

The primary challenge that can keep your body from remaining in motion is injury, and the easiest way to get hurt is to push your body beyond its limits. Injuries often occur when trying to keep up with someone else. Either you find a running or workout partner who is a little more advanced, or just get impatient with your progress and try to push too far too fast. Even if you are young and healthy, everyone has limits, and when you push past those limits recklessly, you will end up with injuries that will prevent you from doing the things you love.

When I first started lifting weights around the age of 13 or 14, I joined a local gym. The place was full of muscle-bound dudes pushing around huge amounts of weight. Of course, I was immediately impressed and wanted to be like them and work toward lifting that kind of weight. The other thing in environments like that is people love to give you advice and tell you the secrets of their "success." I had one guy who told me that the secret to bench pressing more weight was to tighten my weight belt as much as possible, bring the weight down, bounce it off of my chest, then arch my back aggressively and push it up. He was right about one thing; my capacity increased immediately. I also developed back problems that, at the time, I did not understand were related to this ridiculous technique that was designed to move more weight but at the cost of my overall progress.

One day I was in the gym doing bench press this way, when my dad, a little older and a lot wiser than the guy who taught me this technique, saw me and stopped me. He told me to never, ever arch like that. He said I would end up with back problems (which I had already - I did not share this information with him for fear of looking foolish, which I was). Also, bouncing the weight off my chest was a terrible idea and could lead to other injuries. He told me the best way to increase strength steadily is to use weights that push your limits a little, but still maintain control. Bring it down, touch the chest lightly, and press it back up while keeping the back flat on the bench. The long and short of his advice was to operate in a controlled manner within your limits. It may not impress the muscle heads, but you'll avoid injury and ultimately see better progress. Over the next few weeks, I experienced steady gains I had not seen prior, using this controlled technique rather than cheating to obtain a fast result.

Whatever you choose to do that keeps your body in motion, just get out there and do something. Eat healthily, stay hydrated, and operate within your limits. Listen to your body; it will tell you what you need.

<u>Notes:</u>

HEALTH AND WELLNESS

"Anything that's human is mentionable, and anything that is mentionable can be more manageable. When we can talk about our feelings, they become less overwhelming, less upsetting, and less scary."

~ Fred Rogers

First, some general health advice, since there is nothing more important than your health. We just spent a lot of time covering diet, hydration, and exercise, which is one dimension that can help maintain a generally healthy balance and avoid a lot of issues that come along with a bad diet and sedentary lifestyle.

But diet and exercise are not the whole story when it comes to health. Despite your best efforts, anything can happen, and it is vital to stay ahead of all elements of your health to avoid the bad stuff or address the bad stuff quickly if it happens.

The first is regular checkups. If you have the means, regular trips to the doctor and dentist will go a long way toward preventing issues or identifying and correcting small problems before they get bigger. If you or your parents have health insurance, most policies will cover annual checkups and general tests with very little or no money out of pocket. If you do not have insurance, there are community and income-based clinics across the country that provide subsidized healthcare and dental services. It is especially important to get regular dental checkups and cleanings as a young person to ensure dental health and avoid challenging problems down the road. It is very easy to blow this off and wait until problems occur, but that can be costly and cause other issues.

If you cannot get regular checkups and cleanings, you have to take extra care with your personal maintenance and be especially aware of potential problems. The most critical thing with your health, when you suspect a problem, is to act quickly with the help of a medical professional. Seeking out help can be scary, especially if you are sick. It can sometimes feel more stressful to think about seeing a doctor and receiving a diagnosis, getting a bill, or undergoing treatment. But often, issues you experience will not be severe and will be easily treatable. I assure you, if you think you are experiencing a problem and let it wait, rarely will it improve on its own. It is better to get ahead of it, or the treatments can be more extensive, more painful, and more expensive the longer you wait. It is simple for the dentist to fill a small cavity in just a few minutes with minor discomfort. If you wait for months and that cavity becomes large enough, it can lead to other, more severe problems that will be more difficult to correct. Take care of issues early.

Again, even with insurance, visits to the doctor and dentist can be expensive, and there are many community-based options available to you. I have added some resources at the end of this chapter.

In addition to your physical health, you have to pay close attention to your mental health. Life will challenge you consistently with new experiences and interactions that produce many different emotions. I hope that many of the feelings you experience are positive, but the bad ones come too, and, as we discussed earlier - there is the negativity effect. We have a tendency as humans to blow over the good stuff and fixate on the bad stuff, and this can cause some very serious mental issues.

Everyone experiences depression, anxiety, emptiness, loneliness, and if you are experiencing these emotions, you must understand first that you are never alone. Everyone feels the same things. When you start to feel like these emotions are taking over, you must recognize the trend and take some actions to change your dynamic.

Many people will first attempt to self-medicate to cover up the pain with alcohol or drugs, or other bad habits that mask the deeper issues. If you have read to this point, you know my feeling on that one - terrible idea. Just as with any physical problem, if you ignore it or only attempt to cover it up, rarely will it improve. And, with self-medication, you get the bonus of all of the bad stuff I have already covered. I don't have to go over this, again, do I? Don't mask the problem. You need to try to meet your issues head-on.

I will reiterate you must first understand that you are not alone in your feelings, far from it. All people experience the same feelings and emotions, albeit perhaps to different degrees. If you don't believe me, ask around. I have struggled for as long as I can remember with a mix of anxiety, depression, stress, and feelings of inadequacy. There, I said it, and hopefully, a lot of people read it. It even feels kind of embarrassing writing it down and admitting that maybe I am not above such emotions. But I know that every single person who reads this is feeling or has felt the same things. So here we are. Now, what to do about it?

First, try to understand what you are feeling and why. Many of the ancient philosophers who embraced stoicism espoused the philosophy of "sit with it." That is, take a step back and try to determine why you are feeling these emotions. Feelings of depression and anxiety, stress, etc., are human emotions. They are entirely natural and can be beneficial. These emotions are part of the human experience that should be explored and understood. Sit with your problems and see if you can rationalize your feelings and determine the root cause.

Next, if you can understand it, see if you can reframe it. Try to put the emotions in perspective and understand how you can look at things differently. As I write this first edition now, it is the middle of the year 2020, a horrific year for many people, especially teenagers and young adults. Due to the Coronavirus pandemic, many people have suffered weeks or months of isolation and experienced job losses. The stress of avoiding the virus or getting sick can be overwhelming, coupled with the other stressors. The downward cycle here is just beginning as we see increased domestic violence and civil unrest as a secondary effect. Just carrying out a simple task like going to the grocery store seems difficult, and you just get the feeling that everyone is on edge.

Today is one of those times in history in which even the strongest among us begin to wonder how we can possibly survive and come out on the other side. Things seem hopeless, to be honest. But they're not hopeless. In any crisis like we are all experiencing right now, there is always some level of hope and new opportunities that arise. There are new ways of doing things, improvements to processes, new medical treatments, efficiencies to develop. There is a whole world of opportunity hiding within a crisis if you can reframe your thinking around the positive.

If you find that you cannot understand your emotions and cannot effectively reframe them, the next step is to talk about them. Talking about problems is critically important. If you are unwilling to talk about things openly and cannot resolve them, they will continue to worsen. The really big problems begin to occur when these difficult emotions take over, and you find that you are having more bad days than good - more negative thoughts than positive thoughts. You might feel depressed or anxious and try to sit with the emotions but cannot figure them out. You try to reflect or reframe but cannot. Now you feel stupid, or inadequate, or even more alone, misunderstood, depressed, anxious - the list goes on. Sound familiar? Don't try to tell me nobody would understand. You must have the ability to identify and attempt to manage this dynamic.

Like with physical problems, rarely will these issues improve without acknowledging them and making changes or taking actions to correct them, and this could require some help. By talking about your feelings, you will learn that you are not crazy or alone, and, often, others will be able to help you understand and reframe your situation. Having to speak with someone and ask for help does not mean you are weak or inadequate. It means that you are smart and strong for being able to identify your problem and take action. You can start with a friend or adult you trust, then maybe a school counselor or mental health professional, but it is critically important that you take action and not be afraid to admit there is a problem. And don't quit.

If you don't get the answers you need, keep looking.

Unfortunately, many teens and young adults, even many established and very successful adults, never take these steps to seek help and continue to decline mentally and emotionally. Suicide, someone taking their own life, is such an avoidable tragedy that happens far too often. It is sad to see a life end at its own hands when all of these problems are manageable with the right help. If you ever feel like you could hurt yourself in any way, you need to talk to a professional immediately, and I have put the hotline number (800-273-8255) at the end of this chapter, as well as some additional resources. Please don't wait to use them.

While these emotions we are discussing here are all human and often manageable, there are also underlying mental conditions that can contribute to the situation. These underlying problems may make things seem far worse than they are, even totally hopeless, and drive a person to some tragically bad decisions. If you find that you are crossing over from general feelings of sadness or depression to more unmanageable feelings of despair, like there is no hope or no future, you need to talk to someone and get some help right away. Most of these conditions are very common and easily treatable, and there is no reason to suffer in silence or feel any embarrassment in discussing your feelings. No matter how you may think to the contrary right now, the world is a more interesting place with you in it. Get the help you need and stay in the game.

Resources:

The National Suicide Prevention Lifeline provides 24/7, free and confidential support for people in distress, prevention and crisis resources for you or your loved ones, and best practices for professionals. You can call them at 800-273-8255, or go online to https://www.suicidepreventionlifeline.org and chat with a professional.

Community Health Centers — also known as Federally Qualified Health Centers, or FQHCs — provide care regardless of your insurance status or ability to pay. There are nearly 1,400 health center organizations with more than 11,000 locations in urban, suburban and rural communities across the country. They can be found in all 50 states and U.S. territories. Check out https://nachc.org, or https://healthcare.gov to find resources and a location near you.

<u>Notes:</u>

GUNS AND WEAPONS

"I have a very strict gun control policy; if there is a gun around, I want to be in control of it."

~ Clint Eastwood

Guns are practically woven into the fabric of American life. They are more woven in some areas of the country than others. Outside of the States, private gun ownership is perhaps not as common, but not entirely uncommon. At some point in even your younger life, you may encounter a gun at home, a friend or relatives house, or elsewhere.

This chapter does not debate the merits or dangers of gun ownership or gun rights. As with most of the subjects herein, we're going to keep it out of the debatable political realm and stick to the things you need to know to stay safe. Even if you think you will never encounter a gun in your day to day life, please keep reading. These few short rules over the next couple of pages represent most of what you need to know to at least stay safe and out of trouble, and the rules apply to other situations, as well.

Responsible gun owners will always secure their weapons, without fail, and keep ammunition stored separately or locked away, out of the reach of children or inexperienced handlers. Those inexperienced in handling weapons should never even hold them unless being supervised by an experienced adult, in a setting appropriate for training.

Unfortunately, many gun owners are not responsible. They will leave loaded weapons in unsafe places, forego the use of safety or locking mechanisms, or encourage other inexperienced people to handle or even play with them. This dangerous situation can put you, your friends, family, or others at risk.

There are many different types of guns, and we will not even start to go into the different types here because it really doesn't matter. You know what a gun looks like, and you should always apply all of these rules to any weapon you encounter - even pellet or BB guns, or guns you think could be toys. There are so many toy guns now that look very real and real guns that look like toys, and often it can be hard to tell the difference. You cannot take any chances.

Always Treat Every Gun as if it is Loaded

Whether you are holding the gun or someone else is holding the gun, you should always behave as if it is loaded. Point the barrel down at the ground and away from people, and do not even put a finger on the trigger unless you intend to fire. It does not matter if the "expert" who hands it to you or is holding it themselves assures you that it is not loaded. Unless you are capable of verifying it for yourself, you treat it as loaded. A truly experienced weapons handler will make you stick to this rule. Anyone who tells you that you don't need to check for yourself does not know what they are doing and cannot be trusted to keep you safe.

Never Point a Gun at Someone Unless You Intend to Kill Them

That is a strong statement, but it is what certified trainers teach average citizens. Guns are designed to kill, not to play with or make you look cool, or to try to scare someone. Those are foolish games that risk ending in death. Police officers may draw their weapons to de-escalate a situation, and they are trained in that capacity. Other people outside of law enforcement typically do not have this level of training and should avoid similar situations.

If Someone Points a Gun at You, Remove Yourself from the Situation Carefully, but Quickly

You may find yourself on the wrong end of an actual criminal with a weapon or in an otherwise hostile situation. Still, I am more speaking to friends or relatives who are fooling around and either trying to scare you or look impressive. This behavior is not acceptable, and I will say again, you have to assume that the gun is real and loaded, no matter what anyone tells you.

These same rules apply to any projectile or deadly weapon - bow and arrow, crossbows, knives, throwing stars, slingshots, etc. Any of these can become fatal accidents if you ignore these rules. Remove yourself from dangerous situations as quickly and safely as possible, even if it seems like a harmless game or the person is trustworthy. Any responsible, experienced weapons handler will know these rules and abide by them. The inexperienced will ignore them and create unnecessary danger. If you feel that someone is harassing you with legitimate intent to do you harm, notify a law enforcement officer immediately.

<u>Notes:</u>

READ

"Books were my path to personal freedom. I learned to read at age 3 and soon discovered there was a whole world to conquer that went beyond our farm in Mississippi."

~ Oprah Winfrey

Read as much as you can, anything you can get your hands on. Books and other hard copy content are so widely available, easy to find, and mostly free if you know where to look. Reading is a topic that is kind of "do as I say, not as I [used] to do." I learned far too late the joys and benefits of reading. Now that I read as part of my daily routine, I can't get enough.

When I was young, I had every excuse why I could not find the time to read. I would say I did not like reading, or I felt like I was a slow reader, or did not retain information. Reading to me always felt like a challenge. I think this was mostly because I am an impatient person by nature, and taking the time to slow down and absorb information felt like a struggle. I could not get to the end of something fast enough to move on to the next thing.

Reading is like anything else. It takes practice. You're not going to get up off of the sofa and start running 6-minute miles. You're also not going to blow through novels or news articles and retain all of the information on day one. It takes practice, time, attention, and some patience. Even if you feel like you are a bad reader or a slow reader - take the time to practice the reading and the patience that comes with it.

There are so many benefits to reading. When you read, you are gaining perspective and information from authors who have taken the time to formulate their thoughts, organize them, and put them down on paper for you. Today, it is so easy to take an opinion or a sound bite and blast it out over the internet for everyone to read. It is much harder to take that thought and form a cogent argument, thesis, or story and commit it to a book or article.

You can experience places, people, ideas, thoughts that you do not have access to in your daily life. This experience can come in the form of fiction novels or non-fiction books, but even in periodicals like magazines and newspapers. One of my weekly rituals is to read the weekend edition of the Wall Street Journal. I read as much as I can, but I still don't have the time to read as many books as I would like. The Journal's weekend edition has everything from news to opinions, book reviews, food, and travel articles. It is like reading 30 short books in a few hours, with lots of interesting information. The New York Times and other major newspapers also have outstanding weekend editions. Most major newspapers can be found for free through your school or local library and offer student discount rates for a subscription.

Books are also readily available through your school or local library, and little free book exchanges are popping up all of the time in neighborhoods. There are so many exciting things to read, and most are readily available for free or nearly free.

Reading can be both a great escape and a reality check. If you are having a tough time with something, reading a book can take you to another place and time, at least for a little while. It can also provide you with a perspective on your thoughts and feelings or inspire you to take some action.

Finally, this is a little more pragmatic, but reading is the best way to expand your vocabulary and language knowledge. When you see words used in context in print, they will stick with you. So, what should you read?

The short answer is that it is your call. Read what interests you and what you have available. Below is a short list of things I read and why.

Daily Newspapers can help you keep up to date on the latest local, national, and world news, what is happening that can affect us in daily life. Staying ahead of trends and getting ideas for business. Weekend editions of newspapers are an excellent source for travel and recreation, food, thoughts about books to read, profiles of interesting people, and more in-depth reporting and analysis on the world or national news than you might get in a daily article.

Magazines bridge the gap between newspapers and longer books, usually containing articles which are not as timely as a daily or weekly publication, but typically more detailed. You can gain more information and perspective on any number of different subjects. Because magazines usually focus on a particular subject matter, you can dial in on a more targeted analysis or relevant stories based around your specific area of interest, whether it be cooking, sports, travel, nature, or just about anything else.

Fiction can take you someplace else and let you enjoy a story that may or may not be similar to an experience that is even within your reach. Want to experience what it is like to be a spy, or a socialite, or someone living in a different country? Fiction can take you anywhere you want to go.

Non-Fiction can help you learn about a historical event or an interesting person, often with details from the people who were there and experienced them first-hand. Otherwise, researchers have pulled together historical information and aggregated it to give you a real picture of people and events. Similar to fiction, the right type of work can take you to another place and time.

Whatever you choose to read, find something that interests you and just start. When you find something you like, you will be amazed at how far it can take you.

<u>Notes:</u>

VOTE

*"We do not have government by the
majority. We have government by the
majority who participate."*

~ Thomas Jefferson

Any creative or documentary work is influenced at least partially by current events. As I write this, we are about 60 days away from a United States presidential election here in 2020, and if all goes according to schedule, I will publish this book before we see a result. It seems like every presidential election in the last 20 years has been incredibly emotional and hotly contested. This one coming up may burn all of the others to the ground. At least it feels that way now. Most likely, we're heading for a wild ride.

Many modern nations have some voting mechanism for choosing political leaders. The United States is a democratic republic, wherein most key decisions related to laws, taxation, even whether or not the country goes to war, are made by a group of elected officials. The power of the people lies in their ability to select those officials through a voting process.

It is very easy to sit on the sidelines and criticize those in power or their affiliated political parties. It is also very easy for you to exercise your democratic right to vote and make a change.

Voting is a way in which you can personally affect change from the local to the national level. It probably seems like a crazy notion - how one vote could make a difference when, in the national elections, there are over 300 million people in the U.S. But the reality is only about half of the population turns up to vote for elected officials. So, it is still a lot of people, but every vote contributes to the outcome.

Registering to vote can be done online and takes about 2 minutes. Once registered, you will be officially able to vote in any election that personally affects you, from your local districts to state representatives, national representatives, and the President. You can also vote for changes to the law, changes to taxes, and other legislation that directly affects you.

Aside from encouraging you to register and participate, I have only two guidelines for voting.

Only Vote for What You Understand

When you walk into a voting booth or fill out a mail-in vote, you will often have several options. In addition to the people you are voting for, there will be legislative changes, tax changes, and possibly other items that can impact you and your community. Take the time to read and understand what you are voting for and make conscious decisions, don't just push a button or check a box.

Hopefully, when voting for people, you have a good understanding of their level of experience and political viewpoint and can make a decision based upon those criteria. It is more difficult to read and understand legislative changes. Still, local newspapers will publish the specifics in advance, and election officials post them at the local polls where you go to vote. If you need help understanding, it is fine to ask someone you trust to explain it to you. If you don't understand or don't have any basis of knowledge in the selection, it is also fine to skip it rather than just poking a random button.

If You Don't Vote, Don't Complain About the Outcome

I have often joked that the big reason I vote is so I can complain about the outcome if it is not what I like. Many people will try to tell you how to vote, why you are wrong, or why a particular candidate or new tax is terrible. But they won't get off the couch and vote themselves. I do not even entertain commentary from people who are not willing to be part of the process. If you are not willing to inform yourself and participate, you don't have any room to complain about the outcome.

<u>Notes:</u>

SOCIAL MEDIA

"You are what you tweet."

~ Alex Tew, Founder and CEO of
Calm

Social media has a lot of merits, and you probably know more about the platforms and the navigation than I do, so I'll jump right to the core.

Never Post Anything or Send Anything That You Would Not Put on Your Door for Everyone Who Walks by to See

No matter what platform you are on or what promise they make about data retention when you put something on social media or otherwise send it electronically, someone else has access to it, and it never goes away. Someone somewhere is capable of finding it and publishing it for the rest of the world to see. If you put it out there, you had better be sure you want it seen because it will be, and likely by more than just your small, intended audience.

A Large Portion of What you See is Made Up

"Fake News" is the keyword you hear these days, how people are flooding social media platforms with "news" designed to sway your vote or otherwise change your mind about something. It is structured to look like legitimate information from a credible news source. First, you should not be getting any "news" from social media - try the Wall Street Journal, New York Times, BBC, ABC, CBS, or NBC. Even the more politically slanted cable news channels heavily weighted in their opinions generally provide only real news, just with a hefty mix of opinion to color it.

Aside from news, the same holds for everything else. People can hide behind the masks they create on social platforms. So much of what you see is meant to mislead. Many kids, and even many adults, end up being taken advantage of or hurt for believing and following what they read or interacting with the wrong people on social media. Remember our recurring theme here. Don't take everything at face value or believe everything you read. Consider your sources, analyze what you are being told, and look for holes. If something doesn't seem right, take a step back and consider it carefully before putting yourself in an awkward, or even dangerous, situation.

Social Media Linked Depression is Real

I suppose I could do research and cite references to real studies here. I looked through a few papers to see if there is any clinical research backing this statement up, and it is out there. But I don't need research to support what I have seen first-hand. Social media-linked depression is prevalent in teens and young adults, and even in older adults for two major reasons, on two opposite ends of the spectrum, in my opinion.

First, so much of what you read seems too good to be true. Everyone is leading these fabulous lives - traveling, mingling, meeting people, buying cool stuff, while you're stuck grinding it out just to get by and manage your day to day problems. Regularly seeing all of your connections doing all this crazy cool stuff makes your life seems dull and boring in comparison and leads to that depressed feeling. You want to be happy for other people, but it seems like you should be living a better life. The reality is, people are only going to post the cool stuff. Nobody is posting about their money troubles, addictions, abusive partners, or other bad stuff that most people go through every day.

Second, on the opposite side of the shiny, happy posts your friends are making is the negativity that flows rampantly in feeds and comments. I guarantee I can go post, "I hope everyone has a wonderful day," and probably get back 30 negative comments, likely pushing some other agenda. It will be a terrible day because of the liberals, or the conservatives, or aliens, global warming, red meat, or whatever people are railing against at this moment. Maybe people see all the fun their friends are posting, get angry, and then comment elsewhere. Not sure - but either way, you put these two things together, and it can send you mentally into a negative place if you are not aware of the dynamic. So, pay attention to how your social media interactions are affecting you.

Please take it in moderation and remember to be present in the real world. Like everything else, you have to put it down sometimes. Stepping away from social media is especially important when you feel like I have described above.

For some reason, people can't seem to put it down. When at a concert or social event, or even at a park outdoors, it is sad to me to see people flipping on their phones, oblivious to their surroundings. It is like they choose to live in this weirdly fascinating and annoying and depressing alternate reality rather than experiencing real moments in the real world. Choose to make your own life experiences, rather than living through someone else's.

Notes:

HABITS

*"We are what we repeatedly do.
Excellence, then, is not an act, but a
habit."*

~ *Aristotle*

When you speak of habit, people tend to gravitate toward the negative. Smoking, drinking, drugs, sex are all habitual traits that can adversely affect us. They can reel us in and take control, and these habits become hard to break. Humans are indeed, creatures of habit. We like the comfort of doing things the same way, at the same time. Once habits take hold (good or bad), they can be difficult to break.

Here, I want to discuss good habits - those things you can do regularly to help build and maintain your overall productivity. The value of habit, if planned and controlled positively, cannot be underestimated. Once you can slip into a rhythm of doing something positive for yourself, things you might have found difficult or irritating become second nature. You may even begin to enjoy them.

Almost all of this book was written between the hours of 5:30 and 7:30 am. I have a fairly regimented morning routine, not because I have to, but because I have dialed into a few things I enjoy and made them a habit. I wake up, turn on the coffee pot, walk the dog, come back, and fix my coffee. Then I take my computer to the patio and start writing. If I have gotten up with a concept in my head, it comes out easily. If not, maybe I do some editing or research or add some references. Some days, I might write for 2 hours. Some days, 15 minutes before deciding, I would prefer running to writing. It's more about the ritual than the script or even the outcome or work product. Even if I accomplish very little toward my goal, at least I have accomplished something and started the day off right.

Writing is a common habit that many people take on, but you can make any positive action a habit. Anything you establish as a pattern in your life for good will help you start (or finish) each day with a sense of accomplishment and help you make steady progress toward your goals.

What you establish is up to you. Any activity will qualify; writing, reading, exercising, practicing a musical instrument, studying, and even something as simple as flossing your teeth. If you can establish those patterns in your life, even difficult tasks will become easier.

<u>Notes:</u>

DRESS

*"What you wear is how you present
yourself to the world, especially today,
when human contacts are so quick.
Fashion is instant language."*

~ Miuccia Prada

Now, I am not much on "fashion" in the traditional sense. And I am certainly not into expensive clothing designed to impress other people. You will not find me wearing $1000 Gucci shoes, even if I could afford that, which I cannot. Excessively priced clothing works for some. It is what they aspire to, so I'm not casting stones. In fact, there is a place for well-positioned splurgy items like that if it is what you like. The point is, this chapter is not about fashion, per se, more about some tips for navigating how to dress smart and set yourself up appropriately for most situations.

Dress

As the quote from Miuccia Prada says at the beginning of the chapter, your dress is often the first impression you give to people, and first impressions go a long way. You don't have to spend a lot of money or give up your personality to make a sound impression. This principle goes for job interviews, social functions, and even in just day to day life. My intro would suggest you are about to take fashion advice from a cheap hillbilly who has near-zero experience with clothing. This is not far from the truth. Admittedly, I am currently writing this section barefoot while wearing pink shorts and a gray and blue "Ole Miss" t-shirt (true story!). Again, this is not really fashion advice, as it were, but more just general guidelines to help you look your best for most occasions. Even though I am approaching zero understanding of the female wardrobe, the rules generally apply to everyone, and the women I have consulted with on this agree.

First, don't ever be underdressed. Dressing appropriately for a situation is as much for your self-confidence as it is to make an impression. Being dressed well feels good. The designer Kate Spade once said, "Playing dress-up begins at age five and never truly ends." When you have dressed appropriately for an event, you feel like a part of it, not like an outsider looking in. I think I lived the first 22 years of my life underdressed, and it was a constant annoyance that I had no idea how to solve.

On occasion, it is possible to be overdressed, which is typically explainable and not nearly as much of a faux pas as showing up to an event underdressed. I do not recommend attending a wedding or a job interview in a tuxedo unless you are in the wedding party or interviewing for a job as a magician, waiter, or circus ringleader. Other than that, the risk of looking like a goon for being overdressed is small. Guys can always leave the tie in the car, and the ladies can swap the high heels for flats and, boom, instant dress down to match the situation.

Next, when you dress, dress for you but understand your audience. You can maintain your style while conforming to the societal norms of a situation. As I said earlier, don't wear beach sandals to a job interview at the bank and expect to get the job. You can still take some steps to stand out.

Now, you have to arm yourself with at least a few outfits to cover most situations. Casual clothes are easy, and you probably already have that covered. The shorts, t-shirts, sandals, sweatpants, Hawaiian shirts, tennis shoes, ripped jeans, etc.

You need to have a few staples in your closet, and by following a few guidelines, you will be ready for any situation that requires a little more than t-shirts and sweatpants. It would help if you had a few basics that would qualify as a dressy-casual or business-casual, and at least one option for a little more formal. The type of clothes you can use for a function like a wedding, a nice dinner, or a job or school interview. Clothes should fit correctly and be in a generally good state of repair, without holes or other noticeable wear.

One big thing to remember here is that you can cover your bases without spending a lot of money. You don't have to shop at Gucci or Prada (sorry, Ms. Prada, used your quote, but can't afford your stuff) to look sharp and fit right into most situations. Discount stores are a great place to find quality, name brand clothes without paying full retail prices. Major department stores and higher fashion brands will come out with new items for most seasons. When that season is over, they will move their excess inventory out to discount stores like Stein Mart, Marshalls, Ross. The names change from region to region, but the same principle applies. Many stores also have their own outlet stores. At discounters and outlets, you can buy the same quality items you would find in a high-end store, brand new, at lower prices, typically 40-60% off.

Next, big-box retailers like Wal-Mart and Target have plenty of fashionable, reasonably priced clothing from which to choose. You may have to search a little to find what is right for you, but these stores will typically follow the broader-reaching trends in clothing, allowing you to find nice quality items and good prices.

Finally, thrift stores and second hand or vintage clothing stores can often present the option to find exceptionally low prices on just about anything, including big brand names. When I lived uptown in New Orleans, it was a widely known fact that the thrift store on Freret Street was the place to shop for higher fashion on a budget. Many older, wealthy people lived in that area and would donate high-end clothing that was almost new. You could pick up suits for $75 that would cost over $1000 new. When buying on the second-hand market, just make sure that the items are lightly used, not showing a lot of wear and tear, or, if damaged, are easily repairable. Most items can be adjusted for fit, relatively inexpensively, if they are close to your size already. The deals are available to you if you are willing to look for them.

Many people go wrong, not with the clothing choices, but with the fit; too tight, too loose, too short, or too long. I remember showing up to the office one day when I was a young professional, and one of the women who worked there asked me if I had borrowed my dad's coat that day. That was a pretty bad feeling. But it made me self-evaluate, and the coat was definitely too big. It was baggy around the waist and a little too long at the wrist. I didn't even really like the coat and had only bought it because it was cheap. I had found what I thought was a deal and compromised fit for a few dollars - ended up giving it away shortly after that.

You can cinch pants with a belt, but if they are more than an inch or two larger than your correct size, they will look bunched up and sloppy. For guys, pant legs should rest gently on the top of your shoes, with no bunching at the ankle. Shirts and coats should fit around your chest and waist and look natural. Shirt sleeve should come just to the wrist, and coat sleeves should settle just above the crook where your thumb and index finger meet when your arms are at your side. For ladies, I have found through my extensive research there are really no hard and fast rules about length because there are so many more options - different pants, dress, shirt, and skirt styles and situations. It seems really complicated with all of the options, and I am unsure exactly how you all keep up. The most important aspect is that you find the right-sized outfit appropriate for the occasion. Too tight or too loose rarely works for anything. Really, for everyone, look in the mirror and evaluate what you see. If you like your look and understand your audience, chances are they will appreciate how you look also.

Instead of worrying about brand names and buying the most expensive things, worry about matching your look to the occasion and managing fit, and you will feel confident and put together.

<u>Notes:</u>

GET A JOB

One of the greatest feelings in life is landing a job. It may not be your dream job, just something to pay the bills, but being accepted in a job role, any role, is a great feeling. Starting a new position can be a little nerve-wracking but getting into something new and settling in as part of a team is also a great feeling. Over my many years of job searches, and then in management roles where I handled a lot of hiring and firing, I have learned a lot about getting a job (and how to lose one!). I hope to give you some quick guidance here to increase your chances of getting hired when you are ready to go to work. The first step is to get noticed and get an interview. Next, you have to perform well in the interview to get the job offer.

Remember, when you are looking for a job, hopefully, you have something your potential employers want - a specific skill set for which they are willing to pay you. They have something you want - compensation in return for the skills you bring. It is your responsibility to effectively tell that hiring manager why they should hire you, and you should make it as easy for them as possible. Making their job easier will increase your chances of getting noticed, getting into an interview, and ultimately, hired.

Competition for jobs is intense. There are always a lot of people trying to get into a few positions. It is essential that you use care and take the time to get the process right, and you will significantly increase your chances of getting a job offer.

Make a Resume - A Good One

When you apply for a job, you will be applying along with countless other people, and you must be able to get noticed by the hiring manager. In many cases, their first exposure to you will be in the form of your resume. Even if you are a high school kid with zero job experience applying for a minimum wage position, it is good form to have a resume. Your application is your opportunity to tell your potential employer about yourself and why they should hire you. Many jobs will have a scripted application process. You can walk into Burger King and fill out an application that will look like every other application. Leaving a resume along with your application allows you to tell that hiring manager a little more about you - things that are probably not on the application form. Experience you show on your resume if you are young doesn't have to be job experience. It can be grades, or community involvement, or even just a list of things you are passionate about

- as long as it demonstrates your work ethic and is reasonably applicable to the position.

Free resources are everywhere on the internet that can show you common resume formats, and most computer word processing programs have templates built right in that allow you to fill in your information. A few key things grab my attention (positively or negatively) when I screen resumes.

Original, Succinct Introduction

Typically, at the top of a resume will be a section with an objective, career objective, or similar. Many people will use generic language like, "To obtain a job in the foodservice industry that challenges my skills and blah, blah, blah." I tend to prefer something more personal, like an About Me section, that gives a little more insight into the person. What are your real motivations, even hobbies or interests, and how does it apply to this job? Whatever you choose to write, make it personal and honest, not generic.

Clean but Interesting Format

Organize the information correctly and make it easy to read. Colors help a resume stand out if you have the means and clean, easy sections with a reasonably sized text make it easy for us older folks to read.

Use Spell-Check

There is absolutely no reason to have misspelled words in a resume when it is so easy to spell-check and look for errors. It just comes off as sloppy and lazy, and I will typically deposit resumes with misspelled words into the trash immediately. That probably sounds terrible, but it shows that a candidate is not willing to put in the effort to get it right the first time.

The File Name

The file name is so important when submitting a resume electronically, either through a job search engine, a company website or via email. When you save the file, make sure your name is part of the file name. If you save your resume as my_resume.pdf, it stands a good chance of getting lost in the shuffle. If you save it as jennifer_davis_resume.pdf, your name will stand out and be easier for the hiring manager or HR department to save, catalog, and recall.

Applying for the Job

Different jobs will have very different application processes, but there is one constant - make sure you always fill out everything completely, correctly, and honestly. It is ok to be very bold about your experience, but when you start walking the line of embellishing too much, you run the risk of violating trust in the interview process. If the hiring manager suspects that you are less than truthful with your information or level of experience, they will likely not ask you back.

Additionally, filling out everything completely shows the hiring manager that you are thorough and care enough to follow their instructions and provide the requested information. If you do not have an answer for a particular question, fill in the field with N/A for "not-applicable" to at least acknowledge you saw the section and understand it. Here is another secret - "optional" questions are never really optional. I have specific filters set up on my screening processes that immediately move applications without answers to my "optional" questions into the trash. I never even see the application. Again, this demonstrates your willingness to put in the effort. If a candidate is going to do the bare minimum required in the application process, I would expect they will do the same in the job role, and that is not the type of person I will hire.

Make Personal Contact to Get Noticed

This is a big one. Job websites and resume submission engines are an adequate mechanism to apply for jobs. The big challenge with them is the volume of resumes that employers receive. When I am hiring now and have to use job websites to look for candidates, I have to browse through hundreds of totally irrelevant or even halfway complete resumes to find the good ones. Because there are so many, I often rely on the site analytics to point me directly toward qualified candidates. The challenge is for the people who may be young and driven and have a great story to tell but don't have the experience that necessarily aligns with the criteria the website is seeking. You can end up at the back of the line as a result. With many positions, the hiring manager is interested in a person with great integrity and fit with the team more than they are with their experience. Your actual messaging can be a problematic aspect of your application to relay in an online submission.

Sending in lots of resumes through job sites is fine, but a better way to get noticed is through personal introductions and contacts. When I worked for the particularly lousy organization I discussed at the end of the chapter on stress, I was desperate to get away. I used internet job engines and company websites to send in resumes for jobs. I was qualified for many of them, some I was not, but I sent resumes in for probably close to 200 different jobs over three months. Out of all of those applications, I had 3-4 phone interviews. All of them were in different states, and I never did get a single in-person interview.

This strategy was obviously not working. I shifted gears and started making personal contact with people in my contact list and just directly asking for help. I made a phone call to a business development organization and found a gentleman there whose job is to help local businesses grow and keep local talent from leaving the state. I explained that I wanted to stay in the state but must leave if I could not find a technical role. I asked if he knew of anything interesting going on for which I might be a fit. He said he knew a local company that had some interesting projects going on, and he committed to making an introduction. An email and a phone call later, I had an interview. After that one interview, I was hired and able to make the change I wanted.

If you approach the right people with the right message, they will usually be more than willing to help, and personal introductions go a long way.

Nail the Interview

Most interview processes will start with a phone call and then move to an in-person interview. There are a few key things you can do to increase your odds of getting hired.

Be Prepared

There are two primary things you need to be prepared for as any interview begins. First, the interviewer will likely ask you to tell them a little about yourself. You should prepare a brief but thoughtful response that is honest and relevant to the company or position. It is hard for me to provide an example because people and job roles are so different, but I can tell you that when you are sincere and forthcoming, the interviewer will pick up on that. If you are trying to snow them, they will probably pick up on that as well.

Next, and probably even more critical, you need to have done your homework on both the company and your desired position. If applicants fumble through talking about themselves, it is usually ok. I have trouble talking about myself, too. If an applicant has not done any research on the company or the position, I will make small talk for a minute, then end the interview.

I will ask, "Have you had a chance to take a look at the company and what we do?". About 50% of my phone interviews in the past two years ended fairly quickly because the interviewee had not even taken five minutes to look up the company. They had little idea even about the position for which they were applying. Remember, your mission in an interview is to convince the interviewer that you are the right person to fill that job for them. If you are not willing to prepare and cannot even understand the job, you have no chance to describe how your skills align with the job.

Be on Time

Being on time is critical. A professional is taking time out of the busy day to give you a shot at winning a job with their company. You must respect the value of their time. If you are dealing with a phone or online interview, be ready to answer when the interviewer calls or connect early and be prepared if it is a scheduled conference. If the interview is in person, it is advisable to show up 10 minutes early, but not more than 15 minutes early. When I was interviewing in person, I would arrive in the parking lot 30 minutes before the interview time, so I could walk into the building 10-15 minutes early.

Dress Appropriately

Take a re-read of the previous chapter for guidelines, but for an interview, including even an online interview, being dressed well shows the interviewer that you respect them, their company, and their time. It also shows that you respect yourself enough to take the time to look your best. Business casual will suffice for most pre-professional job interviews. However, for guys, you will never go wrong with a coat and tie. For ladies, an outfit of appropriate length with a conservative pattern and nice shoes would work. If you are concerned about being underdressed, as discussed, take it a step further and make sure you are wearing something appropriate. It will also help your confidence in the interview process.

Be Confident, Be Honest, Be Respectful, Be Yourself

Most interviewers are looking for a personality and team fit as much as they are for a particular skill set. This dynamic tends to shift somewhat, the more specialized the positions become as you get deeper into your career, but it remains a critical part of the process. In any event, it is crucial that you put your best foot forward by being open and honest with answers, polite in responses, and demonstrate not only your competency as an employee but your merits as a person. There is nothing wrong with being confident with yourself and with your abilities and communicating this to the interviewer. Answer questions confidently but without arrogance. If you are honest, work hard, and have made a habit of handling your responsibilities, themes we have revisited here repeatedly, you will have no problem nailing an interview and landing a job.

Say Thank You

In a phone interview or phone screening call, make sure you always complete the call by thanking the interviewer for their time. If the hiring manager grants an in-person interview, even a computer-based remote face-to-face interview, always follow up the next day with a thank you. Depending on the situation and how you have established communications to date, an email may be appropriate. You can never go wrong with a hand-written thank you note to your interviewer, thanking them for their time and reasserting your interest in the position. Hand-written thank you notes are becoming a lost art, so they stand out even more. Much more than an email.

One essential thing to remember with a job search is to hang in there and not get too upset or desperate if things are not going your way. Landing a job can be difficult and can take some time, even when you feel like you are doing all the right things. I have been in interviews that I thought I had nailed and never got a call back. I actually had one interview for a technical position, and I was able to fix a computer issue they were having right on the spot they had not been able to resolve, and they never called me again. I joked later that I should have sent them a bill - but like any other relationship, both sides have to feel it, and sometimes it just doesn't work out.

Hang in there, do the right things, and you will land in the right place.

<u>Notes:</u>

WORK ETHIC

"If a man is called to be a street sweeper,
he should sweep streets even as
Michelangelo painted, or Beethoven
composed music, or Shakespeare wrote
poetry. He should sweep streets so well
that all the hosts of heaven and earth will
pause to say, here lived a great street
sweeper who did his job well."

~ Dr. Martin Luther King, Jr.

I must emphasize the value and importance of work ethic. I do not believe this is something one is gifted with at birth but is a learned and practiced behavior. Anyone can work hard if they choose to do so, and those who work harder and smarter will reap the rewards. This chapter is short, but this is a fairly complex subject, some of which we revisit in later chapters related to jobs. It is very simple to state that if you work hard, great things will come to you. Working hard is only part of the story but it is foundational. If you choose not to put an appropriate amount of effort into the tasks you are given, except in extreme luck cases, you will probably not set yourself up for success in whatever venture you are pursuing.

Work ethic is more than just giving the appearance of working hard at something. It is truly dedicating the time you have allotted to focus on the task at hand and work toward successful completion. I have worked with plenty of people who walk quickly around the job site and look stressed and aggravated. I have even heard people say, "man, that guy really works hard and takes this so seriously." In reality, these people have learned to put on a show - looked stressed out, and people think you're "working hard" or "really dedicated." Then they zip back into their office and browse the internet. Projects drag, and people tend to give them a pass, either because everyone assumes they are actually working hard and don't want to offend them or because they are so gruff that everyone is scared to approach them. Trust me; this train runs out of track quickly, and more seasoned managers will pick up on this a mile away and correct it swiftly.

There is no substitution for actually putting in the hard work that you have committed to, and in many cases, someone is compensating you to do. So, decide to be the type of person who will work hard, create value for your employer or team, and generally get things done. Generating great outcomes will often require putting in effort above and beyond that which is expected.

"Make it look easy, but make sure they know how hard it really is." I started saying this many years ago and have used it countless times to coach and train up-and-coming employees. I have also used it to describe how I do things. I practically made a career out of figuring things out behind the scenes and implementing solutions. When I was researching this book, I searched the phrase to give credit where credit is due. I figured this must be attributable to someone, but I cannot find a record of this anywhere, so it could be an amalgamation of other quotes or theories I have drawn from in the past.

Regardless, when I use this phrase, I am talking about longer-term outcomes, not necessarily seeking recognition for day to day activities. You can make things look easy by putting in the hard work behind the scenes that perhaps does not get immediately noticed. It is said that character is defined by how you act when nobody is looking. When you are operating from a place of actual work ethic, the intent to do the best you can to achieve a goal, you don't need day-to-day recognition. Much of the work you do will ultimately be unseen. Achieving your goals may require taking the extra steps to gain an understanding outside of what is directly in front of you to acquire the knowledge you need to succeed and achieve your goal. It might happen after hours or require personal research that you are not even getting paid to do.

Sometimes it may feel as though you are working at a high level, day after day, but not noticed. If you let your work ethic drive your actions and focus on outcomes rather than a need for daily recognition or acknowledgment, the right attention will come at the right time.

<u>Notes:</u>

KEEP A JOB

"Strive not to be a success, but rather to be of value."

~ Albert Einstein

You will more than likely at some point be downsized, furloughed, staff reduced. Let's face it - you're probably going to get fired. I always thought that getting let go from a job was for lazy or inefficient people, and there was no way it could happen to me. I worked too hard, put so much into my jobs, was smart and efficient - there was really no way anyone could let me go. I was 40 years old before it happened, and when it did, I felt like the smallest person on the planet. Now, whether they fired me or I quit - that depends on who you ask. Realistically, if one had not happened, the other would have, so I guess that part doesn't matter much.

In either case, that company and I parted ways. I was back at home for less than 24 hours before my wife informed me that I was bothering her and needed to leave. Not permanently, just during the business day when she was used to my not being around the house grousing about and complaining. So, I called a buddy of mine who had some office space I could use for my job search, packed up a few things, and headed to the office. I was talking with a group of the guys who worked at this office and feeling pretty down for joining the ranks of the devalued and jobless. It was to my surprise that every single person in that room, and collectively this is a brilliant and motivated group of professionals, had been let go at some point. They all had their stories about screwing something up, having it out with a supervisor, or even being in a job over their heads. I was shocked, literally shocked. I instantly felt better about my situation, knowing I was not alone and that it is not uncommon to run afoul of some power structure and find oneself outdoors, so to speak. Let's go over some fundamental principles that will help you keep a job in the professional world.

The Company Can Survive Without You, So Create Value

Do not get lulled into a false sense of security that a company could not possibly operate without you. The company was likely doing fine before you and can make adjustments to do just fine when you are gone. Your position is never safe, regardless of how hard you work or how key your role is, and you must understand your place in the hierarchy. Someone can step in if you leave.

This is all the more reason to structure your work effort around creating value for your employer. Your company is in business to make money, and they pay you to help them. Understand how your role fits into the bigger picture and how the things you can do every day will help accomplish those larger goals.

Get Fascinated

I used to work with a guy at one of my former companies, and he would always say, "What interests my boss simply fascinates me." It is a really unique way to look at an employer/employee relationship and a very accurate one. Pay close attention to what your boss sees as important to the business and get serious about contributing to whatever that is. Of course, most businesses are interested in generating revenues and controlling costs. Other interests could be reporting, safety, efficiency, customer service. There are many different things that your boss may embrace to make the company better and more profitable. Whatever your boss is interested in, get fascinated with it and focus your efforts on higher-level goals. You will make an impression.

Understand the Company Policies

I have seen quite a few good employees let go due to policy violations. In many cases, they broke rules that they were not even aware of. Policies are put in place in companies, kind of like laws for citizens. The policies are there to ensure workers are safe, the company is protected, and rules are enforced fairly across the board. Policy violations, whether intentional or unintentional, informed or uninformed, can end up in job termination. Please pay attention to the published rules and be mindful of them.

Communicate Openly

If you do not understand something, speak up. Sitting silently while a situation deteriorates will only land you in trouble. If you see something going wrong, even if you feel like it is something you should control but cannot, then speak up. It is much better to ask for help upfront and circumvent a problem than to ask for forgiveness once things go wrong, and it is too late.

Work Hard and Pay Attention

Put your best efforts forward every day, remaining focused on creating value and aligning your tasks with your boss' interests. You will drastically increase your chances of not only keeping a job but making consistent forward progress.

Don't Quit Your Job Until You Have Another One Lined Up

There are some good reasons for walking out of a job before you have another one lined up, but they had better be really good reasons. If you're dealing with an abusive or dangerous work environment, it may behoove you to separate as quickly as possible for your safety and sort the rest out later. If you are dealing with minor disagreements, an annoying boss or co-workers, or even just boring or irritating work, make sure you have the next job secured before leaving your current job. Even if you have managed to pull together some savings, finding a new job can be difficult and often takes much longer than you would imagine.

I did this twice, leaving a job before I had another one lined up, and it was a mistake both times. I ran my savings to zero before finding the next job and had to start all over again. Trust me. You can put up with just about anything for a short time while you get your plan together and find what's next for you. Don't let pride or other silly reasons compromise your financial security.

Maintain Savings as a Buffer

Knowing that being downsized, or whatever you prefer to call it, is always a possibility should encourage you first to understand the value of savings. We'll talk about that in more detail here shortly, but anything can happen in the working world, and you have to be ready. The common wisdom is that you should have six months of pay saved in a bank account, and that is typically sufficient to keep you afloat while you look for another job. Put away as much buffer as you can afford to in case the unexpected happens.

<u>Notes:</u>

STUFF

*"The discontent that lies in the human
condition is not satisfied simply by
material things."*

~ Derek Walcott

The famous comedian George Carlin used to perform a hilarious routine on "stuff." I wish I could transcribe it here, but don't want to run afoul of any copyright, and that would also not do it justice. Carlin was a master of the show, and his inflection and expressions make the actual performance far funnier than you could ever imagine from just reading about it. You are much better off looking up the video online.

Anyway, the premise is that most people have a fascination with acquiring and keeping their stuff. There are always little piles of stuff. You have to have a house to keep your stuff, and when you get enough stuff, you have to get a bigger house, so you can buy more stuff. As expected, I am not doing this justice, but you get the point.

Having a huge amount of stuff will not satisfy you, and often the thrill of acquiring something new is quickly replaced by the stress of paying for it, maintaining it, storing it, transporting it, and ultimately getting rid of it.

This is mostly food for thought as you start down the road of life and begin to have the means to acquire things. It is tempting to have a lot of really nice things, for whatever reason - to make you feel more in control, to show off your fortunes, or just possess things you feel you might like to own. The only hard and fast rule I will insert here is that you should never buy anything you can't afford. I will cover that piece, debt, in much more detail in the chapter on money. When it comes to owning things, there are two cost elements to consider; the cost of acquisition and the total cost of ownership.

I will illustrate this with yet another real-world example of my ignorance and impetuousness. I decided one day that I needed a boat. I lived in Louisiana near the water, love to fish, and it made total sense. I started shopping around, set my budget at $15,000, and ultimately found the boat I was looking for. Now, I did not have $15,000, so I borrowed it from the bank. Again, much more on this later.

My wife told me just to save the money and when I feel like fishing, use a fishing guide. A guided trip with friends will be under $1000, so even if we went four times a year, and I paid for everything, that's over three years of trips with no other costs. If we split a trip between friends, we could have even more trips. The guides usually put you on fish to catch. They clean everything. It's really easy and fun. And besides, I was so busy I did not have a lot of free time to go anyway, so we would make the most of it when we did.

I had every excuse in the world why this would not work. Primarily, I wanted to be in control of everything. I wanted to go when and where I wanted to, with no planning or restrictions. Also, $1000 a trip was crazy - if I owned my boat, I could go much more often, and it would be practically free. Or so I thought. Honestly, I did not think. I jumped to a conclusion based upon what I thought I wanted and did not evaluate the entire picture. If I had actually thought about it, rather than operating on pure emotion, I would have realized my wife was right.

So, there is the cost of acquisition; what it costs to buy the thing you want. I went to the bank and borrowed the money, bought a nice used boat on consignment from a dealership, and was in business. Remember, I did not create a budget and plan for this, and I did not save the money in advance - I borrowed the money, which meant I really could not afford it to begin with. Now, I also had a monthly payment to make on the boat, which is more money out of my pocket every month.

Next, there is the cost of ownership, for which I had not planned at all. That payment to the bank includes interest, the money I have to give the bank to let me borrow the money I needed to purchase the boat. You have to buy insurance, another monthly payment. At the time, I had a place to park the boat at my house, so I did not have to pay for storage, but I did have to pay for gas and oil. Every time you tow it, gas for your car costs more, and it was a little farther to where I wanted to fish than I had thought. Then, there is the fee to launch the boat at the dock, bait, ice, equipment. There are also batteries that go bad and periodic maintenance on the engine and the trailer - bearings, tires, and brakes. Many things can go wrong, and they all cost money to maintain properly and repair when they break. I soon found that every fishing trip cost me quite a bit of money when you factor in these things. That is money in addition to what I had to pay every month just to own the boat and keep it working.

Finally - there is the stress of ownership, which is one of most significant points. Think about a house full of really nice things. It's fine to have them around, but what if you like to travel? You worry about the safety of your things while you are gone. You have to pay for insurance in case something happens. What if you get a really good job opportunity in another town? Now, you have to either pack all this stuff and move it without breaking it or figure out how to sell it. Having a lot of stuff can cause some undue severe stress and, by the way, you spent your money to get it.

Anyway, let's get back to the boat. Now I had the boat, but my wife was right, did not have a lot of time to use it. There it sat in my driveway. I wrote checks every month to have this thing, which I really could not (1) make the time to use or (2) even really afford to use. I felt like a real idiot.

Additionally, boats are the kind of thing that need to run to stay in good shape. Problems tend to occur if the engine does not run regularly, so now I had additional responsibility. Every two weeks, pull out the hose, charge the batteries and run that engine in my driveway, whether I wanted to or not. I spent a lot of money to be miserable.

There is a saying that the two best days of a boat owner's life are the day they buy the boat and the day they sell the boat. This saying is mostly true and not only applicable to boats. It is because most people make purchases the way I did - buying something they cannot afford and failing to plan appropriately and consider the longer-term impact. Then, ultimately having to rid yourself of the burden.

Fast forward ten years, I decided it was time to buy a boat again. Some fools never learn, they say, but I learned a few things. Now, I had saved the money toward my goal. It took over a year to save up, but I could pay cash and not have a monthly payment with interest expenses. I found a good deal on a nice quality boat, so I knew if I had to get rid of for some reason, I could do it quickly, with minimal loss. I also planned a place to store it, created a budget, and committed to myself that if I could not afford to run it or ever had to ask a friend to pony-up gas money or buy bait, I would sell it immediately. I have had a great time with this boat. I have spent hours out with friends, caught fish, gotten extra time outdoors with my kid. This time, it was a planned investment that I chose to make and had the means to support.

As I write this, it sits in the boat shed with a burned-out bearing and spindle on the trailer. My trailer guy can't find the part. The motor has not run. This is stressing me out a little.

Avoid the trappings of stuff.

Notes:

MONEY

*"Annual income twenty pounds, annual
expenditure nineteen six, result happiness.
Annual income twenty pounds, annual
expenditure twenty pound ought and six,
result misery."*

~ Charles Dickens

Amazingly, secondary education does not typically include comprehensive financial training for teenagers and young adults. Financial knowledge is one of the key areas of life experience critical to early and longer-term success, and educational systems rarely address the subject. Further, learned behaviors with money that take root early can either set a young person up for success or paint them into a corner that can take years to escape.

The trappings of "stuff" can be overwhelming...the newest mobile device, bad-ass gaming computer, fancy meals, a new car. Nice to have, but like everything in life, they come at a price. The price for many is overwhelming debt that can take years to overcome. In this chapter, we will first understand a budget and then discuss avoiding debt, because I believe this is the biggest challenge for most young people and the least understood. Next, we will move into saving. All of these principles kind of go hand in hand, so we will discuss them individually, then pull it back together at the end.

The first step in understanding the management of money is understanding what you can and cannot afford. You can accomplish this by looking at the money you make every month (your income) and what you spend every month (your expenses). The easiest way to understand this is by creating a small chart with your monthly numbers. You must be honest with your numbers to plan this way. If you are spending $400 a month dining out, you need to write it down and be honest, so you can review your numbers accurately.

	INCOME	EXPENSES
Pay from My Job	$2,200	
Rent		$900
Electric and Water Bill		$100
Groceries		$250

School Expenses		$100
Insurance		$75
Eating Out and Coffee Shop		$100
Money Moved to Savings		$200
Totals	$2,200	$1,725
Net Income	**$475**	

You will notice I have added "Money Moved to Savings" as a line in the expenses because you should be putting something in savings every month. More on that later. So, you can see by the chart above, if you stick to your budget and put some money away, you are left with $475 for the rest of the month. This $475 is your planned "net income" for the month. Now, this has to cover anything not in your budget - gifts, travel, medical bills, or other unexpected expenses. You must understand how your money is flowing in and out every month so you can make adjustments and control it.

If You are Spending More Than You Make, You Will Soon be in Serious Trouble

Spending more than you make comes in only one form, debt, which is the root of all financial evil. When you borrow money from someone in order to make a purchase, you have incurred debt. Debt is a problem for a few reasons;

- You now have what is referred to as a liability - that is, you owe something to someone.

- Borrowing money is never free, it always comes at a price, and sometimes at a very expensive price. That price is interest, or the money that the bank or lender will charge you for using their money.

- When you borrow money and cannot pay it back immediately, you will have to make monthly payments. This is an additional expense every month that now will eat into your Net Income, leaving you with less at the end of every month.

There are many common forms of debt. Some people use bank loans to start a business or make a major purchase, like a house or a car. Loans enable you to purchase things you can't afford with cash. There is a place for this, usually in a business setting, when there is a plan to invest the money to make more money and quickly pay off the debt.

I'm not going to focus on that here. I want to discuss specifically the one major thing that will get you in big trouble quickly - credit cards. Credit cards are relatively easy to obtain and even easier to let slip out of control. When they slip out of control, the financial impact to you can be disastrous. When you use a credit card or any loan, that loan will have an interest rate or the amount you have to pay to hold onto the money you borrow.

With credit cards, the interest rate is usually very high to extremely high for young people with no credit history. Say you get a credit card with a 15% annual interest rate. That means, if you use their money and don't pay it back for a year, you will owe them the money you borrowed, plus 15% of that money. For example, if you use a credit card with a 15% interest rate to buy a TV for $2000, and you do not pay down that $2000, at the end of the year, you will actually owe the credit card company $2,300. At the end of year 2, if you have made only minimum payments, you will owe $2,645. And that debt will continue to grow until you can pay the money back – *all of the original money plus the interest.*

Additionally, the entire time you owe them money, you will have to make some payment every month. So, if you already are having trouble paying the bills every month, you just added one more bill to the mix.

Let's look at a real-world example of how this could affect you. We'll use our basis for this as the first chart and change the next chart up a little by just summarizing the expenses, then adding the credit card debt.

	INCOME	EXPENSES	CREDIT CARD DEBT
	$2,200	$1,425	$2,000
Credit Card Minimum Payment		$50	
Interest Charge			$25
New Credit Card Balance			$1,975

Net Income	**$425**		

So, let me explain what you are looking at in the chart above. You borrowed $2000 from the credit card company to buy your TV. They are charging you 1.25% of the outstanding amount every month (15% for the whole year). In this case, it means $25 per month. They also require you to make a minimum payment of $50.

Now, your "net income," or what you get to keep every month, is reduced by the $50 you use to pay that minimum. And you will notice that you paid the credit card company that $50, but it only reduced the total money you owe by $25 because of the $25 interest charge added to your balance due.

I hope you can see where this is going. You bought a $2000 TV that you really could not afford using credit. Now, you are just making minimum credit card payments on that loan to get by, and after just the first month, your total bill for that TV is already $2,025. If you were to continue this trend of making minimum payments on this TV purchase, it would take you a little over five years to pay off this loan, and the total interest charge will be about $900. So - you have reduced your monthly take-home pay, created the stress of another payment, and you are going to end up paying $2,900 over a five-year period for TV that was originally worth $2,000.

I hope you don't break the TV by accident in year three because you will spend the following two years continuing to pay off the debt for an item you can't even use. The credit card company does not care what happened to your TV, only that you owe them money.

Negotiating Out of Your Debt

You'll see these commercials on TV - "what the credit card companies don't want you to know." They tell you that you can just negotiate out of your debt for "pennies on the dollar." It sounds so simple - I can run up a big tab and then just hire someone to get me out of it for a little bit of money and walk away. I hope you have been paying attention to what you have been reading in this book so far. If you go into any project with a mindset toward getting out of your responsibilities, you are setting yourself up for trouble. When you borrowed the money, you committed to pay it back, and your first goal should be living up to your responsibilities, not wiggling out of them.

And, does it sound right to you that a major credit company will just let everyone walk away from most of their debt? Not a very good business model. You should know by now that everything comes at a price. You might be able to cut some deal and pay the credit card company a little less now, but that will likely severely damage your credit. That means, when you get a little older and maybe go to buy a house, your interest rate could be many points higher than if you had made your payments in full. This negotiation could cost you *hundreds of thousands of dollars* over the life of a house loan. When you duck your responsibilities, you always trade that short-term gain for longer-term pain.

Never Charge Anything on a Credit Card That You Cannot Pay Off in the Same Month, or in a Really Short Period of Time.

There is a place for credit cards, as long as you understand the risks and manage them. I use credit cards frequently for travel or major purchases, mostly because of the insurance benefits. Some credit cards will insure purchases in the event of damage or defects. Most credit cards also offer some level of protection against fraud, so they can be more secure than using a bank card, especially when shopping online. You just have to be mindful of what you are spending and make sure that it fits your budget.

Finally, there may be times when it does not fit into your budget, like an emergency situation where you have to extend yourself a little. If you incur debt, make it a priority to pay it off as quickly as possible. As those balances grow, they become harder and harder to pay down.

Forget About Rewards

Credit cards will try to lure you in with the promise of cash back or travel rewards. These can be considered when *choosing* a credit card but are not a reason for *getting* a credit card. If you are carrying large balances on credit cards and making big monthly payments, you will spend way more money to support the debt than it is worth in "rewards."

We've talked a lot about the bad side of interest, when you borrow money, and the interest works against you. We can now flip over to the good side of interest, where it can make you money. Interest gain comes as a function of savings.

Start Saving Early

Save as much as you can, as early as you can. Getting into that habit of savings early in life will pay you immense dividends later in life. You can open a savings account with a parent or guardian's help at any age and begin to build savings. Savings accounts at most banks are free of charge and will pay you a little bit of interest. More important than interest earnings at an early age, is just starting to build savings and creating the habit of saving. Getting paid for a job, maybe some cash or checks for birthdays and graduations or special events. Take a little bit and tuck it away in your savings.

I'm not going to get too far into this, except to say that the earlier you start saving, the more you will build and the more options you will have in the future. Saving at least a little bit out of each paycheck or each gift you receive will pay you back faster than you expect.

When you get into the working world, many companies offer 401k savings programs. A 401k is a way of saving your money, usually tax-deferred, and companies will often match your contributions up to a certain percentage. That means you can put away, say 4% of every paycheck, without paying taxes on your income, and the company you work for would then also deposit the same amount for you. So if you put $20 from your paycheck into your 401k savings account, the company you work for would also put in $20. It's free money - and it grows without having to pay taxes on it until you withdraw it, which will hopefully be many, many years into the future.

Remember how, when the credit card companies charge you interest, it ends up costing you a lot of money, really quickly? You end up paying a lot more for an item than the original sales price, like that $2000 TV that becomes a $2900 TV? Well, when you earn interest on your savings, it works the same way, but in your favor. The very famous investor and billionaire Warren Buffet made 90% of his wealth after the age of 65. What Mr. Buffet learned early was the value of savings and compound interest. He began saving and investing his money at the age of 10, and over time, it grew to an immense amount.

Here is an illustration of how money can grow over time if you start early. I will use a very simple example, with a very standard interest rate for earnings. The stock market typically earns, on average, about 6-7% rate of return year over year. If you put away just $100 per month and can earn a very conservative rate of return of 5%, in 10 years you will have contributed $12,000 of your own money, but with interest paid to you, it will be worth $16,000. Compound interest is magnificent because as your money grows, your basis for the interest calculation grows. Now, you are earning interest on the $16,000, not just the $12,000 you put in.

If you keep contributing that $100 per month, after 25 years, you would have contributed $30,000 of your own money, but it would be worth $60,000 - that is double what you put in. After a 50-year period, you would have contributed $60,000, and it would be worth $250,000 - more than four times what you put in. So, you see, the earlier you can begin saving, the larger it will grow over time.

Investing

Investing is far too complicated a subject to get into here. You are probably better off getting a secure bank savings account and starting your savings journey at your age. Investing in stocks and bonds and other funds can have risks, and you should never start investing without doing a lot of studying and understanding those risks. For now, get in the habit of building your savings and avoiding debt, and when you are ready to start investing, you may have a nice little bit of money to start working with. If you are interested in investing, I put some suggestions for resources in the last chapter, and you should do a lot of reading and research before starting to invest in anything other than savings. Investing can have many risks if you go into it uninformed, and you don't want to do something silly and lose all of that money you have saved.

Money and standards are a funny thing. There are some strike-it-rich stories out there, and there are some people who were in the right place at the right time or made a ridiculously good deal and nailed it. In most cases, for most people, money comes slow with hard work and leaves fast. As you grow and develop, your standards will change. If you are not careful and aware, this can lead to bad money decisions that you may end up regretting and living with for many years.

I had a discussion one day with my very first boss out of college. He was a successful Ph.D. and entrepreneur, running several different companies. I was working as a design engineer at one of his medical device companies. I cannot even recall how the subject came up or why he was even in the conversation, but I said something like, "If you gave me one million dollars right now, I would never have to work again." He said, "Why do you say that?" I told him that just the interest alone on one million dollars, at that time was like $50,000 a year, which was way more than I would ever need to live. Mind you, he was paying me $18,500 per year (remember my rough GPA in college?), so $50,000 per year meant to me that I would have almost three times as much annual income, and for doing nothing.

He told me that I was completely wrong. I was incredulous - a twenty-something know-it-all. How could I possibly be wrong? Three times my annual income would set me up for life, right?

His argument was, and I will never forget this conversation, "because your standards will change". He said, "If I gave you a million dollars right now, what would you be? You would be a millionaire. As a millionaire, would you live in the same rental house and drive the same truck? No, your standards would change. You would buy a nice house, trade up your truck, everything would change and when it does, you will need more money to support it."

He was 100% right. I did not understand then, what I so clearly understand now, that stuff does not make you happy or secure. Living within your means does. But for many people, chasing the next level defines everything they do, and it becomes a lifelong obsession.

In this instance, my financial advice was coming from a guy with multiple houses, a giant sailboat, and a Porche. The exact person who would know about putting on airs and trying to impress people.

In retrospect, my argument was silly not for the part about making money off of interest, but for saying I would not have to work anymore.

Today, my argument would be, "If you gave me a million dollars right now, I would reinvest it conservatively and keep working my butt off. Let that money grow like it never happened and keep doing what I am doing - which is working hard and keeping to a reasonable budget."

Understand how your money moves, start saving early and don't get caught up in the trappings of major purchases that require debt. Avoid debt, especially credit card debt, and you will have a great start toward a life of financial freedom.

Notes:

TOO GOOD TO BE TRUE

"A fool and his money are soon parted."

~ Thomas Tusser

There is an old saying, something like, "If it sounds too good to be true, then it probably is." Not sure who to attribute that to, but it merits consideration in any exchange of money or resources. When you are young and looking for something, you are especially vulnerable. People who understand this dynamic will seek to exploit your desires or your drive.

When you are young and ambitious, or even young and lazy - you're always looking for something to improve your situation. That something might be more money, more education, more control, a better title, respect from peers, respect from elders. Whatever it is, when the opportunity is presented to you to get that something the fast and easy way, sometimes that can cloud your judgment from the realities or risks of the situation.

I had just started my first consulting company, and I only had one anchor client. I was struggling to grow my business and find new clients when I met an older couple in a joint meeting. This couple had another business and were interested in partnering with my client. They had developed an industry-specific piece of software that filled a niche gap. They had been using it successfully with their company and were looking to expand. We hit it off and talked a bit, along with another software engineer working on the project. The week after the initial meeting, the four of us exchanged emails about some things they wanted to do with their company, and we ended up setting up an in-person meeting.

I made the hour drive across town to their compound and went into the meeting angling to get them signed up as a new client. At the time, I was just a startup and they were a smaller shop that had some tangibles in a solid growth market. If I could help them coordinate the last phase of their development and get the software into some major companies in the area, it could take off, and they needed the help. The meeting started off normal enough, but it did not take long before the meeting's premise shifted into the couple, basically giving the software engineer and myself the company. They had grown the company some but were getting older and had made some money. They had no kids to leave it to, so they would let us continue developing the software suite and phase-out and just give the company to us to run.

At that time, for me, this ticked all my boxes; ownership, title, software development, business development, in a growth market. This business was something I could take on and make my own. I also really liked the software engineer. He was savvy, and I could see him as a good partner. We talked more about the opportunity, and I left the meeting pretty excited. I started thinking about the conversation a little more throughout the hour's drive back home, and some concerns began to arise.

I went home and reviewed my notes from the meeting. Of course, I took notes - always takes notes of critical points in meetings and catalog them for future reference. Some things started to concern me. Primarily, the most obvious question was why this couple was gifting a company to someone they had talked to twice for a total of two hours (me) and the engineer who had worked on their software before, but with whom I gathered they were not particularly close on a personal level. My ego might have led me to believe I am just that impressive, but once I shook off that fallacy, I start to dial in and think more clearly. I called the engineer and just asked him point-blank if he thought that the meeting was odd. He agreed that it was a strange twist that he did not expect and was not quite sure what to make of it. Validation number one that something might be off here.

Aside from this moving quickly and taking this odd turn, I started to think about what it means to own a company. If this couple just handed us the company, signed over the paperwork, and the engineer and I became the new owners - we would get everything related to the company and be responsible for it. We would take on the assets of the company (the good stuff...the money, property rights, customers, branding). We would also take on all of the liabilities (the bad stuff...primarily the debt). Could it be possible that they racked up a ton of debt and were trying to offload the responsibility to pay it, by simply "gifting" the company to myself and the engineer? Software development is not cheap, and as a small company, it is possible that they ran up a tab. So, I wrote a comprehensive follow-up email with a summary of our conversation and several questions, including how much debt the company was carrying. They responded, answering every question except the one about debt.

Very strange, so I just asked them point-blank - how much debt is the company carrying? I never got a straight answer to this very direct question, so I just broke off communications. There were other issues with the deal, but the fact I could not get a straight answer regarding an important financial aspect made me decide this was not something I would choose to pursue.

"If it sounds too good to be true, then it probably is" is not a hard and fast rule, the operative word being probably. The truth is, crazy opportunity can come knocking at any time, and if you are smart and careful, you can capitalize on it. Many people have become very wealthy and very successful by accident because that "too good to be true" was actually true. Could that older couple have really had their hearts in the right place and been trying to set up the engineer and me for success? It's possible, but I will never know. I am ok with that.

The advice here is always to evaluate your opportunities carefully. Look for the risks, look for ulterior motives or ways that people could take advantage of you, and ask authoritative and specific questions. Don't be afraid to challenge a premise either directly or through your internal evaluation. Perhaps that old adage should be rewritten. "If it sounds too good to be true, then it may be, so spend extra time evaluating more carefully by moving slowly and asking probing questions."

Notes:

BALANCE

*"The best and safest thing is to keep a
balance in your life, acknowledge the great
powers around us and in us. If you can do
that, and live that way, you are really a
wise man."*

~ Euripides

As we start to wrap things up here, I just want to quickly
address life balance. It is critical as you go through school
and enter work life to maintain some sort of balance. I
have always been one to take things to extremes, to double down
on a job or a project, and let everything else in my life slip into the
background.

I missed out on some really good stuff in my late teens and
early twenties, and even later because I wrapped myself up so tight
in jobs or projects, I could not see what else was going on around

me. I did not take enough time to maintain relationships, explore new places, or expand my knowledge in some new areas. I would come up with ideas or things I wanted to do but then let them slip away because I did not take the time to establish the balance I needed to accomplish them.

Much is said about work/life balance, and this is where most people get caught up. They get so dialed into work that they forget about everything else. It can also happen with school, family, church, social causes, really anything that is an important part of your life. You have to see when one element of your life is taking over and impacting everything else negatively or preventing you from partaking in other rich life experiences.

I wish I had a formula for you, and to be honest, I still have not figured this out entirely myself. What I have been able to learn is how to identify the dynamic and try to change it. My company will not go bankrupt if I take a day off and go fishing. I may simply do a little extra the following week to catch up or a little more in advance to prepare. My family will not suffer if I have a work emergency and have to stay late and miss dinner, but I'll hang around a little longer at breakfast to balance that out, before racing back to the office.

As I said earlier, there are very few split-second decisions that you will ever have to make. Hopefully, you don't even have to make any. You must identify what is important to you in your life and make time for it, regardless of the other responsibilities you have. Understand when you need to put in a little extra effort in some areas, and maybe pull back in others to balance it out.

<u>Notes:</u>

TOOLS OF THE TRADE

*"The best investment is in the tools of
ones' own trade."*

~ Benjamin Franklin

Well, my friends, I am afraid that our time together here is drawing to a close. I have reached the end of my notes, and hopefully, we have covered some relevant topics that you have found helpful. As I said earlier, learning is a lifelong journey, and I will encourage you to keep reading, keep researching. Never stop trying to improve.

Take in as much information as you can, consider your sources, and develop your own informed opinions. Nobody will look out for you better than you, so do your best to maintain your balance, think for yourself, and make the right choices. When things go wrong, don't throw up your hands and quit. Reframe your thinking, double down, and work harder. Nothing in life worth experiencing comes easy, and you can rectify most mistakes.

I have included below a short list of reference materials I have found particularly useful to me in developing my ideas and opinions and providing some assistance where needed. I hope they are helpful to you, as well. Take care of yourself.

Find a Newspaper

Get into the habit of reading the news every day. I prefer the Wall Street Journal at the national/international level, and also a local news source. Even news aggregation websites can provide a good comprehensive overview of what is going on in the world, and they are mostly free. Having a daily basis of knowledge about what is going on in the world around you can provide solid foundational knowledge and keep you informed as it goes to risks and opportunities.

7 Habits of Highly Effective People, by Steven Covey

This book is a very traditional business text one might refer to as a business self-help book. First published back in 1989, it is a very straightforward read and the principles apply to most facets of work and life.

The Motley Fool Investment Guide for Teens: 8 Steps to Having More Money Than Your Parents Ever Dreamed Of, by David and Tom Gardner, with Selena Marajian

The Motley Fool began in the 90s as a resource for investors, with advice and a very witty and direct writing style. The Motley Fool continues today as a website, with resources online, in podcasts, books and articles. This book is a great place for young adults to begin understanding the core principles of money. Especially the first four chapters, which contain some basic principles and highlight some financial pitfalls. Beyond those first chapters, you can dive much deeper into understanding of investing and different types of investment avenues.

The Art of Manliness

A Website and Podcast may sound like a strange add here, but I have found this one particularly useful. The tagline on the landing page of the cast is "Intelligent conversation, life-improving insights, and actionable advice without the fluff and filler", and that is exactly what this is. Don't be scared by the "manliness" thing, the content is for everyone. Interesting guests and topics, book recommendations and thoughtful insights. At least two of the books on this list I have read after learning more about them from the AoM Podcast. The articles on the site are always intriguing and the cast is available on most podcast platforms and at www.artofmanliness.com/podcast.

Who Will Do What by When?: How To Improve Performance, Accountability and Trust with Integrity by Tom Hanson and Birgit Zacher Hanson

This book is what you might call "business fiction", but the story is illustrative of how making commitments and sticking to them can change your dynamic. This book as become *de rigueur* in many business-training circles, yet it is a very easy read in this story format. It will make you think about how you are handling your commitments, and some changes you can make to build your performance, accountability and trust.

Meditations, by Marcus Aurelius

This collection is a series of writings by the Roman Emperor, Marcus Aurelius, from around the year 167 A.D. This was never intended to be a book, per se, it is actually just a collection of notes he wrote to himself based upon evaluation of his stoic philosophies. The work contains wisdom about a number of topics and some historical recollections of parts of his life. Central to the book, is the theme of carefully analyzing yourself and others, and being able to look at the big picture, seeing things holistically for what they really are. The English translation is available for free through the online library at MIT:

http://classics.mit.edu/Antoninus/meditations.html

How to Write the Perfect Resume: Stand Out, Land Interviews, and Get the Job You Want, by Dan Clay

This is a very comprehensive guide to resume writing and constructing a resume that gets noticed. There are any number of books out there that dole out advice on this subject, but this one is relatively new and aligns with the way I review resumes. It is also straightforward and contains a number of free resources. Beyond just simple resume content and construction, it also covers subjects like explaining gaps in job history, so it will be useful for you from just getting started, to later in your professional career.

Start Finishing: How to Go From Idea to Done, by Charlie Gilkey

I may have never finished writing this book, had I not read Start Finishing. This book is very direct and provides not only some guidelines to completing projects, but also some hard truths about why things don't get done in the first place. If you find yourself struggling to complete projects or develop upon ideas, this one is worth a read.

The National Suicide Prevention Lifeline

The National Suicide Prevention Lifeline provides 24/7, free and confidential support for people in distress, prevention and crisis resources for you or your loved ones, and best practices for professionals. You can call them at 800-273-8255, or go online to https://www.suicidepreventionlifeline.org and chat with a professional.

Locating a Health Center

Community Health Centers — also known as Federally Qualified Health Centers, or FQHCs — provide care regardless of your insurance status or ability to pay. There are nearly 1,400 health center organizations with more than 11,000 locations in urban, suburban and rural communities across the country. They can be found in all 50 states and U.S. territories. Check out https://nachc.org, or https://healthcare.gov to find resources and a location near you.

Addressing Tobacco Addiction

The Truth Initiative (https://truthinitiative.org) provides research and resources, facts and analysis on issues surrounding tobacco and even some other substance abuse. Just reading the information and document disclosures on how these large corporations try to manipulate people, especially young people, will definitely make you angry enough to prevent you from starting. It might even give you the motivation to quit if you are already hooked.

The National Domestic Violence Hotline

National Domestic Violence Hotline (https://www.thehotline.org) or 1-800799-7233 is staffed with advocates available 24/7/365 to talk confidentially with anyone experiencing domestic violence, seeking resources or information, or questioning unhealthy aspects of their relationship.

The National Sexual Assault Hotline

RAINN is the National Sexual Assault Telephone Hotline. Calling 800-656-4673 will connect you with a trained staff member from a sexual assault service provider in your area. They route calls based upon the first six digits of your phone number or your zip code, and do not store your information.

The Substance Abuse and Mental Health Services Administration

SAMHSA's National Helpline is a free, confidential, 24/7, 365-day-a-year treatment referral and information service (in English and Spanish) for individuals and families facing mental and/or substance use disorders. 1-800-487-4889 or https://samhsa.gov/find-treatment

<u>Notes and Other Resources:</u>

Final Thoughts:

ABOUT THE AUTHOR

Lon K. Riley is a father, husband, business owner, and author, educated at Tulane University and the University of Texas at Austin and currently living in Lafayette, LA. Mr. Riley knows a little bit about a lot of stuff. He is just a regular guy trying to reconcile the past, figure out the future, help a few folks along the way, and generally keep from screwing it all up too badly. He wrote this short bio himself in the third person, which he finds both amusing and mildly creepy.